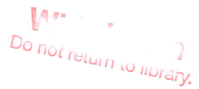
THE GOSPEL IN THE GOSPEL

MEDITATIONS ON
THE BELOVED PARABLES OF LUKE 15

BY

...ER

E

RESS
RGINIA

First printing 1997

The author and publisher have made exhaustive efforts to obtain permission for every source quoted in this book and to insure the accuracy of the material quoted.

International Standard Book Number: 0-941092-33-X
Library of Congress Catalog Card Number: 96-079128

Printed in the United States of America

Cover design by Sharon Harms, Image Associates

Mountain State Press
c/o The University of Charleston
2300 MacCorkle Avenue SE
Charleston, WV 25304

This is a Mountain State Press book produced in affiliation with The University of Charleston, Charleston, West Virginia. Mountain State Press is solely responsible for editorial decisions.

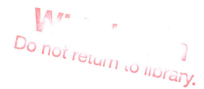
THE GOSPEL IN THE GOSPEL

MEDITATIONS ON
THE BELOVED PARABLES OF LUKE 15
BY
SAMUEL ROBERT WEAVER

FOREWORD
BY
JOHN N. GLADSTONE

MOUNTAIN STATE PRESS
CHARLESTON, WEST VIRGINIA

TO MY WIFE

MABLE

FOR FIFTY–TWO YEARS

MY COMPANION ON THE WAY

CONTENTS

FOREWORD

There are two questions I have kept before me throughout my ministry. One is from Thomas Carlyle: "Who, having been called to be a preacher, would stoop to be a king?" Not I, to be sure! The other is from John Knox who, riding the swell off St. Andrews, looked up from his galley oar and saw the place where "God first called me to the dignity of a preacher." Inspiring words for all of us who have responded to the call to preach, who believe in preaching and gladly spend our one life in the sacred task of communicating the grace of God to a waiting world.

The dignity of a preacher! We are not dismayed by the grave-diggers who for years have gathered round the pulpit, confidently asserting that preaching is finished and nothing can save it from death. For the whole of my ministry preaching has been under the sentence of death but I have had a wonderful time preaching for over forty years! In spite of these gloomy prognostications the Apostolic logic is still shiningly true: "How are men to call upon him in whom they have not believed? And how are they to believe in him of whom they have never heard? And how are they to hear without a preacher?" (Romans 10:14). Again: "It pleased God through the folly of what we preach to save those who believe" (1 Cor.1:21). Colin Morris has just published an excellent book *Raising the Dead.* In it he writes: "As a matter of crude statistics, this coming Sunday hundreds of thousands of sermons will be preached from pulpits in Britain; many millions throughout the world. They may be good, bad or indifferent but they will happen. And in spite of decades of experimentation with drama, dance, dialogue, over-the-garden-wall type chats and twin-pulpit debates, the honest-to-God sermon still bears the main weight of Christian discourse. And in a form that has remained remarkably consistent over the centuries."

The author of the book *The Gospel in the Gospel* shares the dignity of a preacher. Robert Weaver loves preaching and knows how to preach, ministering to great congregations in the United States and Canada. He also knows how to write. The studies he offers no doubt began as sermons, and they are impressive and moving. The printed word, of course, cannot adequately convey the forceful personality of the preacher, the thrust of personal conviction, the pauses and gestures, and the atmosphere of a worshiping congregation which is the proper context of a true Sermon, but every chapter here will provide rich devotional reading for all of us and refreshing examples for every preacher. It is a privilege I cherish to commend this volume.

The studies in this book are models of homiletical craftsmanship. Robert Weaver is a workman who needs not to be ashamed. Every chapter is carefully researched, constructed and presented. There is no hint of what Helmut Thielicke called contemptuously "the slovenly defeatist handing out his weekly chore." What a meticulous preacher and writer Dr. Weaver is! His introductions are grippingly interesting; his illustrations are fitting and imaginative; his endings summarize and drive home the main theme. We have a glorious gospel and it should be communicated with all the artistry we can command.

The studies in this book are soundly biblical. They are written by a Servant of the Word. At the same time it is clear that Robert Weaver reads widely in theology, biography, history, novels, sermons and magazines. Because Jesus is Lord, the best of every branch of human achievement and literature is embraced and used to his glory. It is a splendid idea to write and preach sixteen studies of Luke's beautiful chapter fifteen. I wish I had thought of the idea first!

The studies in this book lift up Jesus Christ in all the fullness of his stature. The Christ we encounter in these pages is no mere teacher with a gift for telling immortal stories. He is both man and God, the Word made flesh, the crucified Saviour and the risen Lord. James Denney once wrote in a letter: "I do not believe that the Christian religion, let alone the Christian Church, can live unless we can be sure of three things: a real Being of God in Christ, the Atoning Death and the Exaltation of Christ." These things are all present in this volume for it is written by a believer who knows the Saviour intimately.

The studies in this book demand a verdict. To be sure, they provide instruction, guidance and encouragement. But they do more than that. They persuade. They convince. As Jesus told parables in order to make women and men think for themselves and come to a decision in a particular issue, so here we are confronted with the Gospel in the Gospel, good news that demands to be welcomed and accepted in a personal commitment to the Christ who is the Gospel.

"To him who loves us and freed us from our sins by his blood, and made us to be a kingdom and priests to serve his God and Father—to him be glory and power for ever and ever! Amen" (Revelation 1:5,6 NIV).

John N. Gladstone

Minister Emeritus
Yorkminster Park Baptist Church
Toronto, Ontario, Canada

PREFACE

According to Luke, Jesus spoke in parables. That is our warrant for using the language of the street rather than the language of the study, for in New Testament times parables were "word pictures," which the Jewish mind could both visualize and comprehend. On the other hand, our Lord's use of parables should warn us against looking there for interpretations that are either artificial or contrived, for parables were "weapons of controversy struck off in the heat of the moment" and their real import is the insight and understanding which they evoke in the listener's mind.

In the following chapters I have tried to keep these observations in mind and if, in the providence of God, these "readings" of Luke 15 prove helpful to some by way of instruction, guidance, encouragement or persuasion, I shall be amply rewarded for the work which I have done in preparing them.

My gratitude to Dr. John N. Gladstone for creating the splendid "Foreword" to this volume. My thanks are due to my son Wayne for reading the original manuscript and offering constructive comments, to my son-in-law, Larry, for checking some elusive references, to my son Murray for resetting the manuscript after I had done the best I could, to Helen Carper, my editor, for her encouragement and assistance, and to my wife for her unfailing support not only in this project but across the years.

ACKNOWLEDGMENTS

Grateful acknowledgment is made to the following writers and publishers for permission to quote works cited:

Scripture quotations from the Revised Standard Version of the Bible, Copyright 1946, 1952 and 1971, by the Division of Christian Education, of the National Council of the Churches of Christ in the USA. Used by permission.

T & T Clark for the excerpt from *The Galilean Accent,* Edinburgh, 1926, by Arthur J. Gossip and for the story from Hastings, *Great Texts of the Bible*, Edinburgh, 1912.

Morris West for the quotation from his book, *The Shoes of the Fisherman*, Nashville, The Parthenon Press, 1952.

Simon & Schuster for the reference from *Memoirs of Childhood and Youth*, New York, Macmillan, 1963, by Albert Schweitzer; for the quotations from *The Parables of Jesus*, Revised Edition by Joachim Jeremias, translated from the German by S.H. Hooke, Copyright © 1954, 1963, 1972 by SCM Press, Ltd.; for the story from *Best Sermons*, edited by G. Paul Butler, Copyright 1952, by Macmillan Publishing Company; Copyright renewed © 1980, by G. Paul Butler; and for the story from *The Radiant Life*, by Rufus Jones, copyright 1944, by Macmillan Publishing Company; Copyright renewed © 1971 by Mary Hoxie Jones.

Westminster John Knox Press and The Saint Martin

Press for excerpts from *And Jesus Said*, Philadelphia, 1970, and from The Daily Study Bible Series, "The Gospel of John," vol. 2 (1956), and *The Letters to the Galatians and Ephesians* (1958) by William Barclay.

The Logos Productions Inc. for the quotation from the *Pulpit Digest*, March/April, 1973.

Abingdon Press for the illustration from T.Cecil Myers, *Thunder on the Mountain*, Nashville, 1965, and for the testimony of Andrew Duncannon from F. W. Boreham, *Wisps of Wildfire*, New York, 1924.

The SCM Press for the explanation of *segullah* from G.A.F. Knight, *Law and Grace*, London, 1962.

The Broadman Press for the excerpts from C. Roy Angell, *Bakets of Silver*, Copyright 1953, Renewal 1981 (All rights reserved) and from *Iron Shoes,* Copyright 1953, Renewal 1981 (All rights reserved).

Harper Collins for the stories from Helmut Thielicke, *The Waiting Father,* Cambridge, James Clarke & Co. Ltd, 1978 and from *Man in God's World,* New York, Harper & Row, 1963.

Manna Music Inc., 35255 Brooten Road, Pacific City, OR 97135, for the right to use lines from "How Great Thou Art." Copyright 1953, S.K. Hine. Assigned to Manna Music, Inc., Renewed 1981. All rights reserved. (ASCAP).

The Epworth Press for Dostoievsky's dying statement to his family, from F.W. Boreham, *The Prodigal*, London, 1941.

Review and Expositor, vol. 80 (Winter 1983), for the humor of Carlyle Marney from John J. Carey's article, "Marney and the Southern Baptists."

George Truett Rogers for an incident from his youth taken from a sermon, "You Are Accepted," April 1984.

Judson Press for a story told by Robert D. Dewey from

The Adult Class, July 23, 1973, Copyright © American Baptist Board of Education and Publication, Valley Forge, PA, 40.

Cambridge University Press for excerpts from John S. Whale, *Victor and Victim,* Cambridge University Press, 1960. Reprinted with the permission of Cambridge University Press.

TITLE ORIGIN

We proceed to consider a parable . . . containing within itself such a circle of blessed truths as abundantly to justify the title, *Evangelium in Evangelio*, which it has sometimes born.

Richard Chenevix Trench
Notes on the Parables of Our Lord

There is no chapter of the New Testament so well known and so dearly loved as the fifteenth chapter of Luke's gospel. It has been called "the Gospel in the Gospel," as if it contained the very distilled essence of the good news which Jesus came to tell.

William Barclay
The Gospel of Luke

Part One

THE PARABLE
OF THE LOST SHEEP

What man of you, having a hundred sheep, if he has lost one of them, does not leave the ninety-nine in the wilderness, and go after the one which is lost, until he finds it? And when he has found it, he lays it on his shoulders rejoicing. And when he comes home, he calls together his friends and his neighbors, saying to them, "Rejoice with me, for I have found my sheep which was lost." Just so, I tell you, there will be more joy in heaven over one sinner who repents than over ninety-nine righteous persons who need no repentance.

Luke 15; 4-7

Chapter One

THE GOOD SHEPHERD

The figure of the shepherd was a common sight in the land of Palestine. Writing about him, George Adam Smith says "On some high moor across which at night the hyaenas howl, when you meet him, sleepless, far-sighted, weather-beaten, armed, leaning on his staff and looking out over his scattered sheep, everyone of them on his heart, you understand why the shepherd of Judea sprang to the front in his people's history."[1] Shepherds were despised by the Egyptians but they were honored by the Jews.[2] So while David was a shepherd lad, keeping his father's sheep, Samuel called him and anointed him king over Israel and it was from that humble beginning that the word *shepherd* climbed steadily until it reached the throne and became a title of kingship.

It is a long way from the sheepfold to the king's court but even that does not tell the full story of this word's triumphant advance for it marched on until it became a designation for God Himself. Thus in the Scriptures He is spoken of as "the shepherd of the sheep" (Hebrews 13:20). The Psalmist says of Him, "The Lord is my shepherd" (Psalm 23:1), and the prophet Isaiah writes, "He will feed His flock like a shepherd, He will gather the lambs in His arms He will carry them in His bosom, and gently lead those that are with young" (Isaiah 40:31). Then, when Jesus appeared He took that figure of the shepherd, added to it His own insights and understandings, and called the finished portrait, "The Good Shepherd" (John 10:11).

In that portrait Jesus pictures the Good Shepherd as one who loves the sheep. The Jews understood that, for in Bible times the relationship between the shepherd and the sheep was much closer than it is in our country. Sheep in Palestine were kept for their wool, not for killing. For that reason they often remained in the flock for anywhere up to eight or nine years, and because of this long and intimate association the shepherd came to love his sheep. He learned to distinguish between them and to appreciate their individual characteristics and their distinctive personalities.

Indeed, in a medium sized flock, the shepherd called many of the sheep by name. Arthur Gossip tells us that he actually heard that being done in France during World War I. His men had come out of the combat zone for a few days' rest and were waiting to go back. Suddenly, coming down a little lane, Gossip saw a shepherd boy, not driving his flock but walking on before them. From time to time he stopped to call one of the stragglers who, hearing his name, came at once and rubbed his body against the shepherd's leg. "So," adds Gossip, "they moved on, and over a little ridge, and out of my life."[3]

Something of that intimacy is reflected in Nathan's description of the love which a poor man had for his one little ewe lamb. "He brought it up and it grew up with him and with his children; it used to eat of his morsel, and drink from his cup, and lie in his bosom, and it was like a daughter to him" (2 Samuel 12:3). Good shepherds loved the sheep of their flock. Sometimes they did things which may appear cruel to us but, even then, it was for the good of the sheep. Thus one Scottish shepherd was sorely tried by the frequent misadventures of a wild lamb. It gave him more trouble than all the rest of the flock. It seemed to be incorrigible. So one day the shepherd took that lamb and deliberately broke its leg. Cruel shepherd? Not at all for, having broken the leg, he carefully set it again, tenderly bound it up, and then lovingly carried the helpless creature in a sling around his shoulders. Day after day the shepherd gave the lamb food and drink with his own hand and when the healing was complete and the lamb was placed on its feet again, it proved to be the shepherd's closest follower. It never left his side again.[4]

The Old Testament uses that theme of the shepherd's love to tell us that God loves the sheep of the house of Israel. He guides them in their wilderness wanderings: "He found them in a desert land, and in the howling waste of the wilderness; He encircled him, He cared for him, He kept him as the apple of His eye. Like an eagle that stirs up its nest, that flutters over its young, spreading out its wings, catching them, bearing them on its pinions, the Lord alone did lead them" (Deuteronomy 32:10-12a). He provides for their recurring needs. "He fed you in the wilderness with manna . . . that He might . . . do you good" (Deuteronomy 8:16). He disciplines them in the furnace of affliction. "Behold, I have refined you, but not like silver; I have tried you in the furnace of affliction" (Isaiah 48:10). And in the end He draws them to Himself. "I have loved you with an everlasting love: therefore I have continued my faithfulness to you" (Jeremiah 31:3). God is the Shepherd of Israel and He loves the sheep of His flock!

Jesus takes that Old Testament picture of God and adds to it the fact that God's love is not confined to Israel, to the descendants of Abraham, Isaac and Jacob, but that it reaches out to the whole flock of humanity. He loves both Jews and Gentiles, both the righteous and the unrighteous, both saints and sinners, both you and me. Indeed the occasion that provoked this parable of the Lost Sheep was the indignant protest of the Pharisees that "this man receiveth sinners and eateth with them" (Luke 15:2). The Scribes and Pharisees called those who did not keep the law, "the people of the land," and refused to associate with them in any way.[5] "That is not like God," says Jesus. "The Good Shepherd loves not only the sheep of the house of Israel, He loves the whole flock of humanity. His love includes us all!"

> God loved the world of sinners lost
> And ruined by the fall,
> Salvation full at highest cost,
> He offers free to all.[6]

"God so loved the world that He gave His only begotten Son, that whosoever believeth in Him should not perish but have everlasting life" (John 3:16).

Jesus pictures the Good Shepherd as one who loves the sheep of His flock and as one who seeks for that which is lost. For the Jews that was something new. In the words of Claude Montefiore, "The Good Shepherd, who searches for the lost sheep and reclaims it, is a new figure."[7] That becomes apparent when we realize two things. The first is that the Old Testament knows nothing of forgiveness for those who are not Jews, that is, for those who stand outside the covenant relationship. In a great verse Micah exclaims, "Who is a God like Thee, pardoning iniquity and passing over transgressions for the remnant of His inheritance? He does not retain His anger for ever because He delights in steadfast love" (Micah 7:18). With God there is forgiveness but, in the Old Testament, it is confined to the members of the house of Israel. The second thing to note is that even among Jews there was forgiveness only for those who sinned through ignorance or weakness. For those who deliberately rebelled against God and turned defiantly against His will, there remained nothing but "a fearful prospect of judgment" (Hebrews 10:27). From those two things it is obvious that the God of the Old Testament is not one who seeks for sinners. He may pardon the penitent when He returns but He does not actively seek him out.

It was Jesus who added the seeking quality to the portrait of God. "What man of you," He said, "having a hundred sheep, if he has lost one of them, does not leave the ninety-nine in the wilderness and go after that which is lost until he finds it?" (Luke 15:4). That is not speculation or wishful thinking but the very stuff of history for Jesus came as the Son of God "to seek and to save that which is lost" (Luke 19:10). God did not wait for the lost sheep to find their way back to the fold but went forth "after that which was lost, until He found it" (Luke 15:4). As Kiril Lakota says in Morris West's *The Shoes Of The Fisherman,* "The Good Shepherd seeks out the lost sheep and carries them home upon His shoulder. He does not demand that they come crawling back, draggle-tailed and remorseful with a penance cord around their necks."[8] That is the good news of the Gospel! That is the great compassion and the wondrous mercy of our God!

Shepherds seek their wandering sheep
O'er the mountains bleak and cold;
Jesus such a watch doth keep
O'er the lost ones of His fold,
Seeking them o'er moor and fen:
Christ receiveth sinful men.[9]

One thing more needs to be added to this picture of
God, for Jesus portrays the Good Shepherd as One who lays
down His life for the sheep (John 10:11). Human shepherds
often did that, not intentionally, but in the defense of their
flock. Thus David risked his life when he fought the lion and
the bear. In different circumstances others have actually
given their lives for the sheep. Thus the story is told that out
on one of the great sheep ranges of the Northwest a shepherd
was left at a very lonely station in charge of a large flock of
sheep. He lived in a little cottage that was fitted with all the
necessary comforts of life. There was no other home
anywhere near. The shepherd, Hans Neilson, lived there with
only his dog Shep for company. After he had been there for
some two years there came a dreadful winter. The shelter for
the sheep was poor. New shelters were planned for the
following spring but nothing had yet been done. It was hard
work for Hans but he succeeded in saving all the sheep until
the last and most violent blizzard of all. Then the wind blew
and the snow fell for three days. After it was over help was
sent from headquarters to see how Hans had fared. They
found his dead body near the sheepfolds and his dog standing
guard over his master but the sheep were alive and well!
"The Good Shepherd giveth His life for the sheep."[10]

The prophets took that theme of vicarious sacrifice and
applied it to the Jewish nation. They declared that Israel had

suffered not only for her own sins but also for the sins of mankind. In "the furnace of affliction" she was refined for greater service. In the words of Bernhard Anderson, "As iron is tempered by fire and shaped on the anvil, so God recreated His people through suffering so that they might be a more effective instrument of His sovereign purpose in history."[11]

The prophets stopped there but Jesus went further. He applied this principle of vicarious sacrifice to God Himself. He pictured the Good Shepherd as one who lays down His life for the sheep. And that is the message which, as Christians, we preach. In James M. Barrie's *The Little Minister* there is a moving scene where Rob Dow gives his life in an attempt to save Gavin Dishart and Lord Rintoul. They are marooned on an island that has been washed away until it is only a little bigger than a chair, while round them sweep the raging waters of the flood. Rob Dow jumps toward the island with an improvised rope in his hand. He does not jump to them, for fear they will be knocked into the water, but beyond them into the foam. He lays down his life for his friends.[12] And that, says the New Testament, is what God has done, not for His friends but for us who are His enemies. "But God commendeth His love toward us in that while we were yet sinners Christ died for us" (Romans 5:8). "He bore our sins in His own body on the tree" (1 Peter 2:24). "He died the righteous for the unrighteous that He might bring us to God" (1 Peter 3:18). He laid down His life for the sheep!

> Souls of men, why will ye scatter
> Like a crowd of frightened sheep?
> Foolish hearts, why will ye wander
> From a love so true and deep?

Was there ever kindest shepherd
Half so gentle, half so sweet,
As the Saviour who would have us
Come and gather round His feet?

For the love of God is broader
Than the measures of man's mind,
And the heart of the Eternal
Is most wonderfully kind.[13]

Chapter Two

THE NINETY AND NINE

We usually follow Jesus in putting the emphasis on "the sheep that was lost." Think instead of the "ninety and nine." In describing them Jesus has reference, not to the wayward and rebellious sheep, but to those who hear the Shepherd's voice and follow Him. He is thinking of the sheep of His flock!

Traditionally we have thought of the "ninety and nine" as "safely laid in the shelter of the fold" but, according to our Lord's parable, they were left in the wilderness. "What man of you, having an hundred sheep, if he has lost one of them, does not leave the ninety-nine in the wilderness, and go after the one which is lost, until he finds it?" (Luke 15:4). That the shepherd knew there were "ninety and nine" indicates that they had just been counted and that suggests eventide (Jeremiah 33:13). So, at the end of a long day, the shepherd brings his flock back to the place from which they had set out, not to some beautiful fold on a private estate where they were fed and watered, but to a rough enclosure in the desolate hill country. Then, having counted them, and having found that one sheep is missing, he leaves the "ninety and nine in the wilderness"[14] and goes after the one that is lost.

That is the story told by our parable and that picture is true to life. The Good Shepherd does not bring us back each night to the Father's house; He leaves us in the wilderness. In the words of Jesus, "I send you out as sheep in the midst of wolves; so be wise as serpents and innocent as doves" (Matthew 10:16). The Church is not in heaven but on earth. Christ has left us in the wilderness of this world surrounded by temptation and in danger of many a fall. That is what John Bunyan was thinking of when he pictured Christian falling into the Slough of Despond, and being taken by Giant Despair, and lingering in Vanity Fair, and turning aside into By-path Meadow, and encountering men like Timorous, and Mistrust, and Wanton, and Discontent. Christ leaves His Church—the sheep of His flock—threatened by every conceivable peril and ringed round by her enemies—tribulation, distress, persecution, famine, nakedness, peril and sword. He leaves the "ninety and nine," not in "the shelter of the fold" but in the wilderness, so that we live under the threat of danger and in the shadow of death!

> Mid toil and tribulation,
> And tumult of her war,
> She waits the consummation
> Of peace for evermore.[15]

Moreover, being left in the wilderness, we need all the resources we can find. We need guidance because "the devil prowls around like a roaring lion, seeking some one to devour" (1 Peter 5:8). We need strength because we are weak and insufficient in ourselves (1 Corinthians 10:12). We need encouragement because like John Mark, Paul's companion on his second missionary journey, we become discouraged. And we need reassurance because "what oxygen is for the lungs, such is hope for the meaning of human life."[16]

We need all the resources we can find in order to sustain our spiritual lives and the Good Shepherd has made provision for our need. An incident in the life of Albert Schweitzer illustrates that. When he was three or four years old he was taken to church every Sunday. To his surprise he noticed, in a bright frame by the side of the organ, a shaggy face turning about and looking into the church. As long as the organ played and the people sang it was visible but as soon as his father began the sermon it disappeared. "That is the devil looking down into the church," he said to himself, "but as soon as father begins with God's Word, he [the devil] has to make himself scarce." Only much later did he discover that the face was that of Daddy Iltis, the organist, and that it was caused by a mirror located at the organ so that he could see when the minister was at the altar and when he went up into the pulpit.[17]   Schweitzer's insight was based on a misunderstanding, yet it suggests the great truth that when we turn to God in simple, trusting faith, we receive the help that we need. The resources are there and it is a tragedy when we fail to utilize them.

Why, therefore, should we do ourselves this wrong,
Or others, that we are not always strong,
That we are ever overborne with care,
That we should ever weak or heartless be,
Anxious or troubled, when with us is prayer,
And joy and strength and courage are with Thee![18]

The Good Shepherd leaves the "ninety and nine" in the wilderness. He does not leave them alone. He leaves them with His friends. Experts on life in Palestine agree that a shepherd would never leave his flock by itself. If he goes to look for a lost sheep he always leaves his other sheep in the care of shepherds who watch over the flock along with him. Thus William Barclay writes, "In the parable [of the Lost Sheep] the shepherd leaves the ninety-nine sheep and goes off to find the one. When we think of it, that seems the surest way of losing the ninety-nine as well; but we must think of communal shepherds. The sheep were left in their charge while the shepherd went to look for the sheep that had strayed away."[19] The Good Shepherd leaves the ninety-nine in the wilderness, but He does not leave them alone. He leaves them with His friends!

That is the work of the ministry. The pastor[20] is called, not to seek great things for himself (Jeremiah 45:5), not to lord it over the Church (1 Thessalonians 2:6-7), but to serve the needs of the congregation. Thus, writing to the ministers of his day, Peter says, "Tend the flock of God that is your charge, not by constraint but willingly, not for shameful gain but eagerly, not as domineering over those in your charge but being examples to the flock. And when the Chief Shepherd is manifested you will obtain the unfading crown of glory" (1 Peter 5:2-4). It is because we think of pastors in that way that we refer to them as "the under shepherds of the flock," for Jesus Himself commanded Simon Peter, "Feed my lambs" (John 21:15), "Shepherd my sheep" (John 21:16), "Feed my sheep" (John 21:17).

The work of the ministry is a great work but the shepherding of the flock should not be left entirely to the clergy. It is the responsibility of every Christian. "We should bear one another's burdens and so fulfil the law of Christ" (Galatians 6:2). The   Church   recognizes   that   in   the appointment of deacons in compliance with the teaching of Jesus, "Whoever would be great among you must be your servant [literally, your deacon], and whoever would be first among you must be your slave; even as the Son of man came not to be served but to serve, and to give His life as a ransom for many" (Matthew 26-28). Nor does the responsibility stop there for again and again in the New Testament we are reminded of our responsibility for the brethren (1 John 4:20-21).

Our parable contains at least one other great truth. It tells us not only that the Good Shepherd leaves "the ninety and nine" in the wilderness, and that He leaves them with His friends, but also that He brings the lost sheep to "the ninety and nine." "And when He has found it, He lays it on His shoulders, rejoicing. And when He comes home, He calls together His friends and neighbors, saying to them, 'Rejoice with me, for I have found my sheep which was lost'" (Luke 15:5-6).

In religious circles we usually identify "home" with heaven and that indeed is the true home of our souls. After all, "here we have no abiding city, but we seek the city which is to come" (Hebrews 13:14). We are pilgrims on our way to the New Jerusalem. As the Negro spiritual puts it—

Going home, going home,
I'm just going home.[21]

The eternal fold is heaven but when the Good Shepherd brings home the lost sheep, He usually brings him not to the eternal fold but back to the "ninety and nine," back to the Church, back to the under shepherds, back to the Christian

fellowship.   You see that again and again in the New
Testament. When the Good Shepherd brought home the
young Pharisee, Saul of Tarsus, He brought him to Ananias
and eventually to the Church in Jerusalem. When He brought
Matthew, the tax collector, home, and the woman taken in
adultery, He brought them not to the eternal fold but to "the
ninety and nine."

When that happens, how do we   receive them?
Warmly and with enthusiasm or coolly and with reservations?
Some years ago a young man in the community got into
trouble. He had financial difficulties and was caught in the
act of breaking and entering. He was sentenced and
imprisoned. A minister visited him in the reformatory and
while there he made profession of faith and asked for baptism
and church membership after he was released. His request
was taken to the Church deacons and they concurred but as
soon as they discovered that he was serving time the
atmosphere cooled and his application was reconsidered.
That, unfortunately, is not the exception but the rule, a fact
which caused Paul Scherer to exclaim, "Prodigals leave home
because elder brothers stay there."[22]

When the lost sheep are brought home they need to be
made welcome and we who have been freely pardoned and
forgiven by God's grace, should be the first to greet them with
open arms. Rita Snowden tells a story of the war which
reflects that Christ-like spirit. In France some soldiers, with
their sergeant, brought the body of a dead comrade to a
French cemetery to bury him there. The priest, in charge, told
them that it was a Roman Catholic cemetery and that he was
bound to ask, had their comrade been baptized into the
Roman Catholic Church? They said that they did not know,

whereupon the priest   replied that he was sorry but that he could not permit burial in his churchyard. Sadly the soldiers went their way and buried their companion just outside the cemetery fence. The next day they returned to make sure that the grave was all right and to their astonishment could not find it. They knew that it was only six feet from the fence but, search as they might, they could not find any trace of the freshly dug soil. As they were about to leave in perplexed bewilderment, the priest appeared and told them that he had been troubled because of his refusal. "So," he said, "I rose from my bed early this morning and with my own hands moved the fence to include the body of the soldier who had died for France."[23] That is the spirit of compassion and mercy that becomes the followers of Christ, and I would hope that where there are fences you will move them, where there are prejudices you will lift them, and where there are reservations you will let them go. It is to the "ninety and nine" that the Good Shepherd brings the lost sheep and we are untrue to our Lord if we do not make them welcome!

Chapter Three

ON THE HILLS AWAY

There were ninety and nine that safely lay,
In the shelter of the fold;
But one was out on the hills away,
Far off from the gates of gold—
Away on the mountains wild and bare,
Away from the tender shepherd's care.[24]

Those words, written by Elizabeth Clephane and set to music by Ira D. Sankey, are almost a paraphrase of our Lord's words as found in Luke 15. They come alive as one looks at Alfred Soord's canvas for there one sees "The Lost Sheep" clinging helplessly and hopelessly to the edge of the cliff, with night approaching, a storm coming on and the hungry eagles circling nearer and nearer above their unfortunate prey. It is into this desperate situation that the Good Shepherd comes. He digs the point of his shepherd's crook into the mountain's rocky side for support and then, greatly daring, He stretches out His arm "to seek and to save that which is lost" (Luke 19:10). It is a simple gesture but it expresses in a dramatic way the Shepherd's love for His sheep and His willingness to give His life, if need be, for them.

But none of the ransomed ever knew
How deep were the waters crossed;

> Nor how dark was the night that the Lord passed
> through,
> Ere He found His sheep that was lost.[25]

"Not without stirring of heart," says George Buttrick, "can we hear of a shepherd seeking a lost sheep, despising distance and darkness in the search. But on the divine plane the story is like a daybreak."[26] At that level humanity is the flock, and Christ is the Good Shepherd, but who are the lost sheep?

Often they are the adventurous sheep. For too long we have thought of the lost sheep as black sheep, that is, as bad sheep. We have assumed that they were lost because they deliberately forsook the Good Shepherd, but closer association with lost sheep does much to dispel that notion. Some lost sheep are certainly vicious and perverse but far more are lost because, being preoccupied, they lose sight of the Good Shepherd and wander away, whereas the more placid sheep follow the Shepherd wherever He goes. As the nursery rhyme puts it—

> Mary had a little lamb,
> Its fleece was white as snow,
> And everywhere that Mary went
> That lamb was sure to go.

There are people like that. It often takes real courage to follow the Good Shepherd but, on the other hand, there are men and women who do not have enough character to lose their characters. "It often requires a strong character," says Henry Drummond, "to go wrong. It takes a certain originality and courage . . . before a man can make up his mind to fall out of step with society and scatter his reputation to the winds. So it comes to pass that many very mean men retain their outward virtue."[27] The placid sheep keep close to the Shepherd but the more adventurous sheep, following instinct and drawn by this attraction and that, often lose sight of Him and, too late, discover that they have wandered away. They awake to the realization that they have lost their bearings and are caught by forces they cannot control.

Lost sheep are not necessarily black sheep; they may be adventurous sheep, and that is one reason why they are worth recovering. When they have learned through experience and have been restored by the Shepherd's love, they often become the leaders of the flock and the Shepherd's most faithful followers. That is what Thomas Carlyle was getting at when he said, "The world's worth is in its original men. By these and their works it is a world and not a waste."[28] That is a judgment which history bears out. Saul of Tarsus was a persecutor of the Church and the man who held the coats of those who stoned Stephen, the first Christian martyr, but when he was found of Christ he became a preacher of the Gospel and the greatest missionary statesman the world has seen (Acts 8:1,3). Augustine was a roué and a libertine but when the Good Shepherd lifted him up he became the famed Bishop of Hippo and a great defender of the faith.[29] Charles Coulson, a lawyer driven by ambition and the desire for power, became Richard Nixon's "hatchet man" and was sentenced to serve time for his part in the Watergate scandal but when he was found of Christ he established the "Prison Fellowship," a ministry to those behind bars.[30] Lost sheep are not necessarily bad sheep; they are often adventurous sheep and the best of all Shepherds wants them for His own!

It needs to be pointed out, however, that "away on the mountains wild and bare" the lost sheep are powerless to save themselves. When the evil deed has been done it cannot be undone; we have to live with our guilt. When the act has been committed, it cannot be recalled and the burden and shame of it all lies heavily upon our hearts. One thinks of David standing before the prophet Nathan, after committing adultery with Bathsheba and murdering her husband, Uriah the Hittite, and listening as Nathan says, "Thou art the man" (2 Samuel 12:11-10). Or one thinks of Lady Macbeth washing her hands after the death of Duncan, King of Scotland, and crying:

> Here's the smell of blood still:
> All the perfumes of Arabia will not sweeten this little hand.[31]

What's done cannot be undone! We have to live with our guilt! We have to bear our shame! We cannot forgive ourselves!

Moreover, having wandered "away from the tender Shepherd's care,"[32] countless lost sheep have discovered that they are powerless to break the grip of sin. One such man comes to mind. He was kind and generous but he had one besetting sin and that was alcohol. Each time he fell he swore that it would not happen again but it did and in the end he lost both his wife and his business. He was a lost sheep, unable to overcome the habit that cursed his life. Unfortunately the number of those lost sheep is legion.

We have to live with our guilt; we find ourselves powerless to break the grip of sin over our lives and it is a

grim fact of life that eventually we all sit down to a table of
consequences. Having made our beds we have to lie upon
them. Having sown the wind we reap the whirlwind (Hosea
8:7). Having sinned we must face the consequences of our
misdeeds. While conducting a mission in the Stony Mountain
Penitentiary in Canada, John Sutherland Bonnell met a
fair-haired lad who was incarcerated there. The young man
told him how he became a criminal. One of his companions
suggested a holdup and the loaded gun was entrusted to him.
In the course of robbing a drug store things went wrong. The
gun went off and the man behind the counter was wounded.
Then followed days and nights of terror as the young man
waited for the inevitable visit of the police.

One evening, when he was in his bedroom, he heard
the doorbell ring. His father answered and two men walked
in saying, "We have a warrant for the arrest of your son."
Leaning over the stairway the young man heard his father say,
"Gentleman, I am sorry but someone has blundered. It can't
be my boy you are after. Jack is a wonderfully fine fellow. I
am sure he can explain everything." To which one of the
detectives answered, "We can have the explanations later. All
we are interested in now is to get our hands on him!" The
young convict looked at Dr. Bonnell and said, "I knew the jig
was up so I walked down the stairs. My father looked at me
and said, "Jack, tell the officers that there is a mistake. I am
sure you haven't done anything wrong." I had to say to one
of the best fathers that God ever gave a boy, "I am sorry,
father, but they are right. There is no mistake. I was in on the
robbery."[33] At that point the young man was powerless to
save himself. He had to face the consequences of his
misdeeds. So he was convicted and sent to prison.

The truth of the matter is that lost sheep are helpless sheep and, if they are to be saved, the help must come from beyond themselves. And that help is available. Over against our helplessness there stands God's grace. There is One who is able to forgive our sin, One who can break the power of canceled sin, One who can make us more than conqueror in the face of life's frustrations and disappointments. "He is able to do far more abundantly than all that we ask or think" (Ephesians 3:20). In that regard Joachim Jeremias tells us that "when a sheep has strayed from the flock, it usually lies down helplessly and will not move, stand up, or run. Hence there is nothing for the shepherd to do but to carry it, and over long distances this can only be done by putting it on his shoulders,"[34] which he does.

The Church has taken that to mean that there is rejoicing in the heart of the Shepherd, joy in heaven, over one sinner who repents and that is a great truth. It is not that God loves the "ninety and nine" any less but that there is a special rejoicing in the heart of God because the lost is found, because a brand has been plucked from the burning, because the forces of darkness have been defeated.

> But all through the mountains, thunder riven,
> And up from the rocky steep,
> There arose a cry to the gate of heaven:
> 'Rejoice! I have found my sheep!'
> And the angels echoed around the throne,
> 'Rejoice! for the Lord brings back His own.'[35]

It is not only the Shepherd that rejoices, however; there is also joy in the heart of the lost sheep as well. How can he help rejoicing? In place of danger he has security.

Instead of the howling of the wild beasts he hears the music of the Shepherd's voice. For the discomfort of the rocks there is the softness and warmth of the Shepherd's shoulder. And instead of death there is life.

Dr. P. W. Philpott, sometime Pastor of the Philpott Tabernacle in Hamilton, Ontario, tells how one morning about 3 A.M. he was awakened by someone pounding on his door. The man was a complete stranger but he said, "I am come to ask you to go with me to pray for a dying girl." Dr. Philpott went and there, in a house of prostitution, he found a girl still in her teens. It was evident that her hours were numbered. As Dr. Philpott pondered what he should say the girl asked him if there was not a story in the Bible about a sheep that had gone astray and about a shepherd that had gone after it and brought it back. "Yes," he replied, "that is the story of the ninety and nine and about the one that went astray." "The one," murmured the girl, unconsciously putting the emphasis where Christ first put it, "the one that went astray."

Dr. Philpott read her the story of the lost sheep and then, turning to John's Gospel, read about the Good Shepherd who gave His life for the sheep. Then he prayed with that dying girl while the other girls either knelt or stood sobbing around the bed. When he had finished the girl looked up and said, "It is wonderful. The Good Shepherd has found me and He is holding me to His heart."[36] That day there was rejoicing not only in the heart of the Shepherd but in the heart of the lost sheep as well!

And sometimes, blessed be God, there is also rejoicing in the heart of Christ's other sheep as well. There is a postscript to our story. The girl was so happy in her new found joy that Dr. Philpott ventured to go home, but when he returned the next day he learned that she had passed away. One of the girls came up to him, however, and said, "We all wished you had been here when Mary passed away. She was so happy. She kept saying, 'The Shepherd has found me and is holding me to His heart.'"

Dr. Philpott left and the years passed by and one day, preaching in another city, a young woman came to him and with a smile asked, "Don't you recognize me?" Then she told him who she was. "I am the girl," she said, "who told you of Mary's passing that morning and of how happy she was in her new found joy. But there was something else I wanted to tell you as well. Once or twice I started to write but did not have the courage to finish the letter." "Well," said Dr. Philpott, "what is it you wanted to tell me?" She replied, "Just this, that the morning the Good Shepherd brought Mary in on His one shoulder, I came in on the other!"[37]

Chapter Four

MORE JOY IN HEAVEN

Jesus concludes the parable of the Lost Sheep with a description of the Good Shepherd coming home, calling together his friends and his neighbors, and saying to them, "Rejoice with me, for I have found my sheep that was lost" (Luke 15:6). Then he adds this postscript. "Even so, I tell you, there will be more joy in heaven over one sinner who repents than over ninety-nine righteous persons who need no repentance" (Luke 15:7).

What rivets attention there is the statement that there is joy in heaven. Too often, when we think of death and of the life beyond, we think of the great white throne, of the day of judgment and of the lake of fire. That note of accountability is certainly present in the New Testament but the Good News of the Gospel is that heaven is a place of joy. There we are saved from judgment by the death of Christ and there we find no pale copy of our life here but fulness of life, life more abundant, life that is radiant and overflowing.

> They stand, those halls of Zion,
> Conjubilant with song,
> And bright with many an angel,
> And all the martyr throng:
> The Prince is ever in them;

> The daylight is serene;
> The pastures of the blessed
> Are decked with glorious sheen.[38]

Heaven is a place of joy! That is why everything that destroys our happiness is carefully excluded. Thus Peter tells us that our inheritance there is "incorruptible, undefiled, and unfading" (1 Peter 1:4). And John, writing in the book of the Revelation, assures us that there will be "no more tears, and no more death, and no more crying, and no more sorrows, and no more pain for the former things have passed away" (Revelation 21:4).

Heaven is a place of joy! That is why everything that destroys our happiness is carefully excluded. There we will lay aside our earthly bodies with their weaknesses and limitations and there we will be given bodies that will be the perfect instruments of our wills. There we will meet loved ones again. There we will enter into the communion of the saints and have fellowship with the choice spirits of all the ages. And there we shall see Christ, face to face.

> The bride eyes not her garments
> But her dear bridegroom's face.
> I will not gaze at glory
> But on my King of grace!
> Not at the crown He giveth,
> But on His pierced hand:
> The Lamb is all the glory
> Of Immanuel's land.[39]

Heaven is a place of joy!

But if heaven is a place of joy, God must be a radiant Spirit! He must be a happy God! Rufus Jones, the Quaker philosopher, tells of visiting Baron Friedrich von Hugel in London, England. At the time von Hugel was one of the foremost philosophical thinkers in Europe. They talked about many things but eventually the time came to say good-bye. Just before they parted von Hugel said, "Before you go I want to tell you of the four conditions of life which must be fulfilled before anyone can be canonized a saint in my church." Von Hugel was a Roman Catholic. "First of all, he, or as is more often the case, she, must have been loyal to the faith of the Church. In the second place the person must have been heroic. He must have faced danger and difficulty in a magnanimous and unconquerable spirit, and have done what seemed impossible for a person to do. In the third place, the person who is to rank as a saint must have been the recipient of powers beyond his ordinary human capacities. He must have been the organ of higher forces than those which appear to belong to human nature as such, so that an element of the miraculous gets expressed through his life and deeds. And finally, in the fourth place, through good and evil report, through prosperity and the loss of it, in the mountain top experience and in the dull round of everyday life, he must, she must, have been radiant." Then, drawing himself up to his full height, von Hugel said, "They may possibly be wrong about those first three conditions, but they are gloriously right about that fourth condition—a saint must be radiant!"[40] If radiance like that is required of a saint, how much more must it be true of God! God is a radiant Spirit! He is a happy God!

Too often our Christianity does not leave that impression. It is dour and forced, a matter of obligation and duty rather than something that is spontaneous and free, a thing of beauty and a joy for ever! It is G. K. Chesterton who said, "A real Christian who believes should do two things: dance out of the sheer sense of joy and fight out of the sheer sense of victory."[41] That being the case let us endeavor to be real Christians. Let us run away to God and, when we come back, our faces will be lit up and our lives will be radiant. Then those about us will be drawn to Christ rather than being repelled by our representation of Him.

Heaven is a place of joy and even now, says our Lord, God rejoices over the ninety-nine righteous persons who need no repentance. That is a strange way for our Lord to speak, for the Bible makes it crystal clear that we are all sinners. "There is none righteous, no, not one" (Romans 3:10). "All have sinned and come short of the glory of God" (Romans 3:23). "All our righteous deeds are like a polluted garment" (Isaiah 64:6). We are all sinners and we all need to repent. What then does our Lord mean by saying that God rejoices over the "the ninety-nine righteous persons who need no repentance?" (Luke 15:7). He means that there is joy in heaven over those who come to Him before they commit gross sin, before they make shipwreck of life.

We can all understand that. Just as we rejoice over our children who never cause us a moment's anxiety, so God rejoices over the sheep of His flock who never go astray. He rejoices because He knows what they are saved from. He knows that when they hear His voice and follow Him they are saved from many cruel briars and ragged rocks and wild beasts that lie in wait to destroy them. They are saved from shame and remorse and eventually from judgment.

God rejoices over those who come to Him before their

lives are marked and scarred by gross sin because He knows
what they are saved from and what they are saved to. They
are saved to walk in the green pastures of His grace, to lie
down beside the still waters of His comfort, to journey along
the paths of righteousness, to travel unafraid through the
valley of the shadow, to feast at the table of His bounty and,
at the last, to rest safe and secure within the eternal fold.

> Goodness and mercy all my life
> Shall surely follow me:
> And in God's house for evermore
> My dwelling place shall be.[42]

God rejoices over the ninety-nine righteous persons
that need no repentance because He knows what they are
saved from and what they are saved for—life in fellowship
with Himself here and now and beyond that, the glory and the
wonder of the Father's house.

Still further, God rejoices over the ninety-nine because
He knows what they are saved for—lives of usefulness and
service. David started out to be the shepherd of his father's
sheep but when the Good Shepherd called him he followed
until, in the providence of God, he became the shepherd king
of Judah and the sweet singer of Israel. Peter began as a
fisherman on the sea of Galilee but when Christ called him he
went on to become "a fisher of men" and one of the "rocks"[43]
on which Christ has built His Church. Paul could have spent
his days as a Jewish rabbi arguing over the minutiae of the
law but instead, responding to the challenge of the Galilean,
he went out to become Christianity's greatest missionary and
her most inspiring preacher.

There is joy over "ninety-nine righteous persons who need no repentance" (Luke 15:7), that is, over those who come to God before they commit gross sin and fritter away their time and waste their talent and ruin their reputation. There is joy in heaven over all such! We must never forget that. God wants us to come to Him as naturally as a flower opens to the sun. He wants us to turn to Him in the days of youth before our lives are bruised by the sharp rocks and before they are torn by the briars of evil!

There is joy over "the ninety-nine righteous persons who need no repentance" (Luke 15:7). That is a reassuring thought but Jesus adds something more. He tells us that there is even more joy over one sinner who repents. There is more joy over one sheep that goes astray and is brought back by the Good Shepherd than there is over the rest of the flock. That does not mean that God loves the sinner more than He does the saint. He does not put a higher value on bad men than He does on good men. It is certainly part of the glory of the Gospel that God loves us "in spite of our sin" but that does not mean that He loves us because of our sin. To say that there is "more joy in heaven over one sinner who repents than over ninety-nine persons who need no repentance" (Luke 15:7) is not to say that God loves the sinner more than the saint, nor is it to say that God approves of what the sinner does. God is "of purer eyes than to behold evil and He cannot look upon wrong" (Habakkuk 1:13). Moreover, as the writer of Hebrews puts it, "He is a consuming fire" (Hebrews 12:29) to destroy that which is contrary to His will. His face is turned against all unrighteousness and even now He is seeking to build His kingdom of truth and love and purity in our midst.

What does God mean then when He says that "there is more joy in heaven over one sinner who repents than over ninety-nine righteous persons who need no repentance"? (Luke 15:7). He means that God loves each and everyone of us no matter how insignificant we are and regardless of how low we fall. God loves us in spite of what we are. Two young people from New England, a man and a woman, were very much in love before the American Civil War. They became engaged and looked forward to a life together. Then the Civil War broke out and the young man was drafted and went into action. He and his fiancée never missed a day in writing to each other and expressing their mutual love.

Meanwhile in battle after battle the young man was fortunate until the terrible Battle of the Wilderness. The day after the battle the girl went to the mailbox and discovered that there was no letter from the man she loved. Two weeks went by until she received a letter written in a strange handwriting. It read as follows. "My dearest: I am having my friend write this letter to you. You see, in the last battle I lost both my arms. I will be dependent on someone for the rest of my life. I write this letter to tell you that you are as dear to me as ever but, because of my helpless condition, I am releasing you from our engagement."

That very night that young lady boarded a train and headed for the scene of battle. When she reached the army hospital, she inquired as to where she could find her fiancé. She walked down the long row of army cots and when she came to the bed, she rushed over, threw her arms around his neck and said, "These hands will always take care of you. I will never, never, let you go. For, you see, I love you!"[44] So speaks God!

Part Two

THE PARABLE OF THE LOST COIN

Or what woman, having ten coins, if she loses one coin, does not light a lamp and sweep the house and seek diligently until she finds it? And when she has found it, she calls together her friends and neighbors, saying, "Rejoice with me, for I have found the coin which I had lost." Even so, I tell you, there is joy before the angels of God over one sinner who repents.

Luke 15:8-10

Chapter Five

THE SEARCH

"What woman, having ten silver coins, if she loses one coin, does not . . . seek diligently until she finds it?" (Luke 15:8). Those words tell us that human experience, far from being our search for God, is actually God's search for us. In our preoccupation with living and our concern to get ahead most of us give little thought to God. For many, at least during the early years of life, spiritual things seem insignificant and far away while material things are of prime importance. Moreover, in our self-sufficiency, many of us feel little need of God until we experience tragedy or meet with disappointment. Indeed, we are often blind to all that God has done for us and unaware of our dependence upon Him. As a result we make little or no effort to seek after Him.

In spite of that, God, in the greatness of His love and in the wonder of His mercy, searches after us. He seeks us in the torment of our sin, in our sense of failure and in our awareness of guilt. "Wretched man that I am," cries Paul, "who will deliver me from this body of death?" (Romans 7:24). He seeks us in the emptiness and unrest which are the undertone of all our days. "Vanity of vanities," cries the writer of Ecclesiastes, "all is vanity. . . . All streams run to the sea but the sea is not full!" (Ecclesiastes 1:2,7). It is what Augustine had in mind when, looking back over the excesses of his youth, he declared, "Thou hast formed us for Thyself, and our hearts are restless until they find rest in Thee."[45]   Again, He seeks us in the disappointments and frustrations of our lives.   To assume that these things are simply the result of chance or blind fate is surely a mistake. Anyone who has read the story of Joseph or is familiar with the book of Job, or who has stood at the foot of the Cross, knows that there is meaning and significance to those experiences and that, in them, God is seeking us out, endeavoring to teach us that "here we have no abiding city but that we [should] seek the city to come "(Hebrews 13:14).

Still further, God seeks us in the beauty of Christlike characters who make us feel ugly and dissatisfied with ourselves because in them we catch a glimpse of the persons we should be.   So Jacob, looking upon the countenance of Esau, is constrained to cry, "To see your face is like seeing the face of God, with such favor have you received me" (Genesis 33:10).   God seeks us in all these ways and He seeks us in that strange man upon His cross.   Standing there, seeing what our sin does to incarnate love, our hearts are smitten and broken, and we cry:

> O break, O break, hard heart of mine!
> Thy weak self-love and guilty pride
> His Pilate and His Judas were:
> Jesus, our Lord, is crucified.[46]

It is fitting, therefore, that   the recognition of this Divine search come from the pen of an anonymous writer; for you and I feel that if he had not written those words first we would have said something like that ourselves.

I sought the Lord, and afterward I knew
He moved my soul to seek Him, seeking me;
It was not I that found, O Savior true;
No, I was found of Thee.

Thou didst reach forth Thy hand and mine enfold;
I walked and sank not on the storm vexed sea;
'Twas not so much that I on Thee took hold
As Thou, dear Lord, on me.

I find, I walk, I love, but O the whole
Of love is but my answer, Lord, to Thee!
For Thou wert long before-hand with my soul;
Always Thou lovedst me.[47]

Jesus tells us that human experience, far from being our search for God, is actually God's search for us but, when that realization is brought home to us, our first impulse is to flee. You see that in Francis Thompson's poem "The Hound Of Heaven." Like Jonah he fled from God. He went to London as a student but fell into evil ways. He lost his money. He became a drug addict. Indeed he went from bad to worse until he was reduced to holding horses' heads at the curbside for a few cents. Few men have sunk lower than Francis Thompson and later, looking back, he records that flight in unforgettable words—

I fled Him, down the nights and down the days;
I fled Him down the arches of the years;
I fled Him down the labyrinthine ways
Of my own mind; and in the midst of tears
I hid from Him, and under running laughter,
Up vistaed hopes I sped;

And shot, precipitated,
Adown titanic glooms of chasmed fears,
From those strong Feet that followed, followed after.[48]

We do the same thing. We try to escape God by plunging into life. We try to shut Him out by immersing ourselves in work or by plunging into a round of social activities. We let ourselves become so involved that we have no time to think about the meaning of life and destiny. To all such Jesus speaks when He says, "What will it profit a man, if he gains the whole world and forfeits his life? Or what shall a man give in return for his life?" (Matthew 16:26).

At other times we try to escape from Him by assuming the role of spectator. Instead of admitting that we are responsible to God we try to reverse the role and become those who investigate God's claims. We make religion into an intellectual exercise instead of accepting it as a call to commitment and action. Thus, in the story of the Rich Young Ruler, a young man came to Jesus to talk about religion. "Good Teacher," he said, "what shall I do to inherit eternal life?" Jesus, sensing in this approach not an earnest search after truth but an evasion of God's claim, replied, "You know the commandments: Do not commit adultery, Do not kill, Do not steal, Do not bear false witness, Honor your father and mother." When the young man insisted that he had observed all those commandments from his youth up, Jesus, knowing that his heart was still not right with God, said, "One thing you still lack. Sell all that you have and distribute to the poor, and you will have treasure in heaven; and come, follow me" (Luke 18:18-22).

We try to escape from God by plunging into life, by

assuming the role of spectator and by reducing God's claims to a list of legal requirements like Church attendance, or tithing, or respectability because by so doing we avoid God's radical demand for total commitment and full surrender. That is apparent in the case of the Scribes and Pharisees. They limited God's demands to externals, evading those which offended them, until Jesus cried, "Woe to you, Scribes and Pharisees, hypocrites! for you tithe mint and dill and cummin, and have neglected the weightier matters of the law, justice and mercy and faith; these you ought to have done, without neglecting the others" (Matthew 23:23).

Still further, we try to escape God by confining Him to a specific area of our thought or behavior. Thus we acknowledge God's demands on Sundays but not during the rest of the week or we recognize Him as the Lord of the Church but not as the Lord of life. It was this kind of escapism that Amos had in mind when, speaking on behalf of God, he said, "I hate, I despise your feasts, and I take no delight in your solemn assemblies. Even though you offer me your burnt offerings and cereal offerings, I will not accept them, and the peace offerings of your fatted beasts I will not look upon. Take away from me the noise of your songs; to the melody of your harps I will not listen. But let justice roll down like waters, and righteousness like an everflowing stream" (Amos 5:21-24).

When we become aware of the Divine search, our first impulse is to flee, but in attempting to escape God we discover that He is inescapable. That is the story of Jonah. Jonah was told to go and preach to the people of Ninevah, "that great city, and cry against it; for their wickedness has come up before me" (Jonah 1:2). Unwilling to do that, because the Ninevites were Gentiles and he did not want them to repent and be saved, Jonah went down to Joppa and took a ship to Tarshish to flee from the presence of the Lord, only to find that God was the God not only of the dry land but also of the elements. "The Lord hurled a great wind upon the sea, and there was a mighty tempest on the sea, so that the ship threatened to break up" (Jonah 1:4). When those on board cast lots to find out who had offended the Almighty the lot fell upon Jonah. He confessed his sin and was cast into the sea. Then Jonah discovered something else. He learned that God is the Lord of the earth, and the Master of the wind, and the Controller of the sea. "And the Lord appointed a great fish to swallow up Jonah; and Jonah was in the belly of the fish three days and three nights" (Jonah 1:17). Jonah learned that he could not escape God because He is inescapable.

That is the story of Jonah and that was the experience of the Psalmist. He discovered that no matter where he fled God was already there. "Whither shall I go from Thy Spirit? Or whither shall I flee from Thy presence? If I ascend to heaven, Thou art there! If I make my bed in Sheol, Thou art there! If I take the wings of the morning and dwell in the uttermost parts of the sea, even there Thy hand shall lead me, and Thy right hand shall hold me. If I say, 'Let only darkness cover me, and the light about me be night, even the darkness is not dark to Thee, the night is bright as the day; for darkness is as light with Thee'" (Psalm 139:7-12). God is inescapable!

Francis Thompson was driven to the same conclusion.

Halts by me that footfall
Is my gloom, after all
Shade of His hand, outstretched caressingly?

'Ah, fondest, blindest, weakest,
I am He whom thou seekest!'[49]

Francis Thompson learned the hard way. How much
better it would be for us to recognize our insufficiency and
our need of God! How much better for us to realize that He
wants to bless us "far more abundantly than all that we ask or
think" (Ephesians 3:20). And how much better for us to yield
to Him "before the evil days come and the years draw nigh"
when we will say, "I have no pleasure in Him!" (Ecclesiastes
12:1). "Therefore," in the words of Paul Tillich, "don't flee!
Let yourself be arrested and be blessed!"[50]

Chapter Six

THE LAMPS OF GOD

When the woman in this parable discovered that she had lost one of her coins she lit a lamp. The coin was a silver drachma which was worth only a few cents but it represented more than a day's wage for a working man in Palestine and may have been one-tenth of her meagre savings.[51] Even more important than that, it may have been part of a headdress of ten silver coins linked together by a silver chain for at that time the headdress was the mark of a married woman and was almost the equivalent of her wedding ring.[52] Moreover, she lit a lamp, not because it was night but because the low door let very little light into her miserable, windowless dwelling,[53] and the floor of her house being "beaten earth covered with dried reeds and rushes,"[54] looking for a coin there was like looking for a needle in a haystack.

When it comes to looking for the lost coins of humanity we need to know that God has His lamps also. The name of the first is conscience. That is apparent from the story of the woman taken in adultery. You remember how it goes. The Scribes and Pharisees brought a woman taken in adultery, in the very act, to Jesus and reminded Him that according to the law of Moses, she should be stoned. What should they do? "What do you say about her?" they asked. Jesus did not answer but bent down and began to write in the sand. The word which Luke uses in telling the story is not the usual word for *write* but a word that can mean to record something against someone.[55] Thus it has been suggested that Jesus wrote in the sand the sins of which the different Scribes and Pharisees were guilty. "Jonas defrauded a poor man of a pair of shoes." "Eleazor stole a widow's home." "Asaph brought false accusation against his neighbor."[56] There is support for this interpretation in the Armenian translation of the New Testament which reads, "He Himself, bowing His head, was writing with His finger on the earth to declare their sins; and they were seeing their several sins on the stones."[57] At any rate, convicted by their consciences (John 8:9 KJV), they went out one by one until only Jesus was left. Then Jesus, looking up, said, "Woman, where are they? Has no one condemned you?" To which she replied, "No one, Lord." Then Jesus said, "Neither do I condemn you; go, and do not sin again" (John 8:11).

It is difficult to explain the mystery of conscience but the reality of its judgment cannot be denied. As the book of Proverbs puts it, "Man's conscience is the lamp of the Eternal, flashing into his inmost soul" (Proverbs 20:27).[58] In other words, there are some things which we know to be wrong and there are other things which we know we should do, and when we fail to obey that "inner monitor" the accusations of conscience disturb our peace.

The first lamp which God lights as He seeks the lost coins of humanity is conscience, and that lamp needs to be carefully tended for when it is filled, not with the oil of understanding and love but with prejudice and ignorance, it leads to destruction and death. Thus Lecky, writing as a historian, declares that during the Inquisition "Philip II and

Isabella the Catholic inflicted more suffering in obedience to their conscience than Nero or Domitian in obedience to their lusts."[59]   And in his play, *The Deputy,* Hochhuth makes Gerstein say, "Conscience is a treacherous guide. I am convinced that Hitler acted according to his conscience."[60]

The lamp of conscience should be carefully tended and then, having been carefully tended, it should be faithfully obeyed. Otherwise the time comes when, darkened by sin, it no longer provides light and we no longer see the way God wants us to take. Thus when Richard Croker approached the end of his notorious career as chief of Tammany Hall, he was asked if he had any regrets. Removing his cigar from his mouth and thinking for a few moments, he said solemnly, "No sir, not one. I do not remember ever having done anything I ought not to have done, for I have done good all my life."[61]   Such a character must surely have "a conscience wide as hell."[62]   It was to avoid that fate that John Bunyan refused to leave Bedford gaol. "I am resolved," he said, "to stay in gaol until the moss grows upon my eyebrows rather than take my conscience by the throat and strangle it."[63]   For the same reason Martin Luther refused to recant at the Diet of Worms. "I cannot and I will not recant anything," he declared, "for to go against conscience is neither right nor safe."[64]   That applies to us all.

We have said that God has His lamps. If the name of the first is conscience, the name of the second is the Bible. The scriptures can light our pathway because they provide us with a standard by which to measure our lives. That is what Paul is getting at when he says, "Every inspired scripture has its use for teaching the truth and refuting error, or for reformation of manners and discipline in right living"

(2 Timothy 3:16).[65] He can say that because, on the one hand, the scriptures reveal our sin and failure while, on the other hand, they point out the way we should take. You see that in the story of King Josiah as recorded in 2 Chronicles 34. In the eighteenth year of his reign Josiah commanded that the house of God be repaired. In the course of that renovation the book of the law was found.[66] It was read to the king who, hearing it, "rent his clothes" (2 Chronicles 34:19) because he realized the magnitude of Israel's failure. Then, having acknowledged Israel's failure, he led them in removing abomination from the land and in a return to the service of God (2 Chronicles 34:33).

The scriptures can light our pathway because they provide us with a standard by which to measure our lives and because they have power to convict us of our sin. In the words of the writer of Hebrews, "The word of God is living, and active, sharper than any two-edged sword, piercing to the division of soul and spirit, of joints and marrow, and discerning the thoughts and intents of the heart" (Hebrews 4:12). Tokichi Ishii is evidence for that. He was a hardened criminal. He had murdered men, women, and children and was in prison awaiting death. While there he was visited by two women who tried to talk to him through the bars of his cell but he glowered at them like a caged and savage animal. Abandoning the attempt to talk to him, they left him a Bible, hoping that it might succeed where they had failed. He began to read and, having started, could not stop. Indeed he read on until he came to the words, "Father, forgive them for they know not what they do." Those words broke him up. "I stopped," he said. "I was stabbed to the heart as if pierced by a five inch nail; . . . I do not know what to call it. I only know that I believed and my hardness of heart was changed."

Later, when the jailer came to lead him to the scaffold, he found not the hardened, surly brute he had expected but a smiling, radiant individual.[67]

The word of God is a lamp that reaches into the very depths of our beings. That is why it is important for us to read it, not once and not occasionally, but on a continuing basis. "Thy word is a lamp unto my feet and a light unto my path (Psalm 119:105).

God has a third lamp and that is the Church. Certainly any reading of the New Testament makes it clear that God intended the Church to be a light in the darkness of the world and in New Testament times she was such a light. She was a rebuke to sinners. As men looked at the lives of the early Christians they became aware of their own sin and failure. Indeed that is one reason why Paul and his fellow Christians were opposed and persecuted in the book of Acts. On the other hand the Church was a beacon light to those who "hungered and thirsted after righteousness" (Matthew 5:6), for by the witness of her lips and the quality of her life she pointed men to Christ and to the life for which He stood. "God has shone in our hearts," declares the great apostle to the Gentiles, "to give the light of the knowledge of the glory of God in the face of Jesus Christ" (2 Corinthians 4:6).

Today the light of that lamp has grown dim. There are still those whose lives are a rebuke to sinners and an inspiration to the saints but the lives of many professing Christians are quite indistinguishable from those of worldly men. As a result they are poor witnesses for Jesus Christ because there is little evidence of Christian commitment and dedication in their lives. Is that the company to which you and I belong? If it is, we need to rededicate ourselves to Christ and we need to pray with the hymn writer—

> O make Thy Church, dear Saviour,
> A lamp of purest gold,
> To bear before the nations
> Thy true light, as of old.[68]

Like the woman in the parable of the lost coin, God has His lamps—conscience, the Bible, and the Church—but the greatest of them all is Christ for He is the light of the world (John 8:12). As men have stood in His presence they have seen a beauty there that has made them feel ugly.[69] Thus one thinks of Simon Peter on the shore of the Sea of Galilee, falling down at Jesus' knees, saying, "Depart from me, for I am a sinful man, O Lord" (Luke 5:8). Or one recalls Zacchaeus, anxious to make restitution for the evil he had done, declaring, "Lord, the half of my goods I give to the poor; and if I have defrauded anyone of anything, I restore it fourfold" (Luke 19:8).

That, however, is only part of the story, for in the presence of Christ men have not only become aware of their unworthiness but have also been filled with a great and daring hope. In *Pictures That Preach,* Charles Nelson Page tells the story of a rough sailor, from one of the boats that travel the Great Lakes, who came to see Munkacsy's *Christ before Pilate* when it was displayed in Hamilton, Ontario. He confronted the woman who was in attendance at the door of the exhibit-hall with the blunt question, "Is Christ here? How much to see Christ?" When he was told the admission price he growled, "Well, I suppose I'll have to pay it." Then, swaggering into the room, he sat down in front of the great picture and studied it for a few moments. Presently his hat came off. He gazed at it a little longer then, leaning down, he picked up the descriptive catalogue which he had dropped when he took his place. He read it over, examined the painting anew and so remained for a full hour. When he came out there were tears in his eyes and a sob in his voice as he said, "Madam, I came here to see Christ because my mother asked me to. I am a rough man sailing on the Lakes and before I went on this cruise my mother wanted me to see this picture. I came to please her. I never believed in any such thing, but the man who could paint a picture like that—he must have believed in it. And there is something in it that makes me believe in it too!"[70] The greatest of God's lamps is Jesus Christ and we all need to stand in the light of that lamp until the future—our future—becomes bright with the promises of God!

In the parable of the lost coin the woman lit her lamp hoping to find the silver piece which she had lost. In God's case there is this all-important difference. God lights His lamps not for His own sake—He knows who and where the lost coins are—but for our sakes. He wants us to see our need and, when we come seeking His face, He wants us to be assured of the warmth and reality of His love.

In Ian Maclaren's *Beside the Bonnie Brier Bush* there is a moving passage where Flora Campbell is on her way home after a sojourn in the Far Country. Marget Howe, one of her neighbors, has written on behalf of her dead mother, but she knows that no one can speak with authority for her father with his religious ideals and iron principles. If he refuses to receive her it would have been better for her to die in London. Suddenly a turn in the path brings her within sight of the cottage and her heart comes into her mouth for the kitchen window is a blaze of light. For a moment she fears her father may be ill but in the next moment she understands and, in the greatness of her joy, she runs the rest of the way![71]

God has His lamps and when we see them may we, too, understand the greatness of His love and run to Him!

Chapter Seven

NOT WITHOUT DUST

George Buttrick has pointed out that the search for the lost coin was not without dust.[72] In a humble Palestinian home there was no flooring, only the trampled down earth, and the woman's palm leaf broom must have raised a lot of dust if she swept diligently while she looked for her cherished possession. Her search was not without dust!

That is also true of God's search for the lost coins of humanity for God does not hesitate to sweep out our house of life from time to time. That should be evident to all who read history or observe the human scene or who understand the experiences of their own lives. Thus sometimes God disturbs the even tenor of our lives through the sweepings of change. When we are not disturbed we tend to become arrogant, confident of our ability to provide for our own needs, and we are inclined to become insensitive to spiritual things. That is what Jeremiah had in mind when, referring to Moab, he said, "Moab has been at ease from his youth and has settled on his lees; he has not been emptied from vessel to vessel, nor has he gone into exile; so his taste remains in him, and his scent is not changed" (Jeremiah 48:11). That is powerful imagery but its thrust is largely lost because most of us are not familiar with the wine making industry. The process which was followed was actually a simple one. The wine-juice was poured into a great vat and allowed to stand until the lees, the dregs, settled to the bottom. Then it was poured into another container and the process was repeated until the wine-juice was pure and clear. The quality of the wine depended on this repeated emptying from vessel to vessel for if the juice remained on the lees, if it was allowed to stagnate, the contamination of the dregs was communicated to the wine which then became sour and bitter. And that, says Jeremiah, is what transpired in Moab. She had lived a more settled life than Israel and, as a result, she became proud and arrogant, indifferent and insensitive to the unseen realities. That, of course, happens not only to nations but to individuals as well. In the words of the Psalmist, "Because they have no changes . . . they fear not God" (Psalm 55:19 KJV).

When that occurs, God does not hesitate to disturb the normalcy of our lives through the sweepings of change. One thinks of Abraham settling in Haran, enjoying a life there that was comfortable and secure, adapting to the environment that surrounded him. It was a quiet, relaxed kind of existence and Abraham might well have remained there had not God sensed the danger and called him from his country, and his kindred, and his father's house, and sent him out "to look forward to the city which has foundations, whose builder and maker is God" (Hebrews 11:10). Again, one is reminded of Saul of Tarsus settling upon the lees of Pharisaism so that he was in danger of becoming proud and self-righteous. This man, chosen to be the "Great Lion Of God,"[73] was being tamed and domesticated by the dregs of legalism—a fate that would have made him useless as the Apostle to the Gentiles—so God disturbed the even tenor of his life by the goad of the law, by the spirit and confidence of Stephen in the face of death, by the heroism of the Christians whom he persecuted and by the testimony of the empty tomb. Still further, one recalls the Christians of Asia Minor to whom John writes in the book of the Revelation (Revelation 3:1-4). They were conforming to the ways of Rome and, by so doing, losing both their message and their mission. So God allowed them to be persecuted and, purged by fire, they came out pure gold. That should make it clear to all of us that when God sees His children "settling on the lees," He does not hesitate to disturb the serenity of their lives through the sweepings of change.

It is such a sweeping that we see going on in our world today. In the words of Walter Sikes, "What is new about the changes that are taking place around us, among us, and within us, is not change itself; change goes on everywhere at all times.   What is new is the pace of change, the extent of change, and the depth of change."[74]   How true! Indeed, looking at the chaos and confusion of our world, we can sympathize with Marc Connelly in *The Green Pastures* when he says, "Everything dat's fastened down is comin' loose."[75]

Sometimes God upsets the even tenor of our lives through the sweepings of change and sometimes He does it through the sweepings of sickness. The classic example is Job. Job was an upright man. "There was a man in the land of Uz, whose name was Job, and that man was blameless and upright, one who feared God and turned away from evil" (Job 1:1). He was also a religious man. "His sons used to go and hold a feast in the house of each on his day; and they would send and invite their three sisters to eat and drink with them. And when the days of the feast had run their course, Job would send and sanctify them, and he would rise early in the morning and offer burnt offerings according to the number of them all, for Job said, 'It may be that my sons have sinned and cursed God in their hearts.' Thus did Job continually" (Job 1:4-5). Over and above all that Job was a man of faith for even after he was afflicted with "loathsome sores from the sole of his foot to the crown of his head" (Job 2:7), he rebuked his wife for suggesting that he curse God. "You speak as one of the foolish women speak," he declared. "Shall we receive good at the hand of God, and shall we not receive evil?" (Job 2:10). Job was a man of genuine piety but his goodness was encrusted with pride. Instead of recognizing his indebtedness to God he felt that God owed him something—health and wealth and happiness! So God tested Job, an experience that shook him to the very depth of his being, but the result was a more mature faith and a better understanding of the ways of God with men!

Is there nothing of that in our experience? We go along day after day, caught up in the mad scramble for things, confident of our ability to make our way and with little thought for either God or for eternity. Then God lays us low. He takes us out of circulation. He puts us in a hospital bed. He gives us cause to reflect so that often we see life differently and change our ways.

Still further, sometimes God disturbs the even tenor of our lives through the sweepings of sorrow. That is what Taylor Caldwell has in mind when in *Prelude to Love* she tells the story of Caroline Ames. Brought up in poverty and seeking for security Caroline makes money her God. Then, suddenly and unexpectedly, her daughter Elizabeth becomes sick and dies. Her son develops a brain tumor that threatens to destroy his sight and even cause death. Caroline's life is disturbed by the sweepings of sorrow! They prove, however, to be the workings of God, for out of those tragic events there came a new sense of values, a fresh vision of life, and a renewed faith. "I will lift up mine eyes unto the hills, from whence cometh my help. My help cometh from the Lord, which made heaven and earth. . . . The Lord is thy keeper; the Lord is thy shade upon thy right hand. . . . The Lord shall preserve thee from all evil; He shall preserve thy soul. The Lord shall preserve thy going out and thy coming in from this time forth, and even for evermore" (Psalm 121 KJV).

When His human coins are lost God does not hesitate to sweep out our house of life and that sweeping often stirs up quite a dust. Sometimes it stirs up the dust of our anger. You see that in the story of Namaan the leper. Afflicted with leprosy, he follows the advice of his wife's servant, and seeks out Elisha the prophet. Instead of coming to the door to greet him, Elisha sends a messenger to say, "Go and wash in the Jordan seven times, and your flesh shall be restored, and you shall be clean" (2 Kings 5:10).

Namaan is incensed at this affront to his dignity and rank and he goes away saying, "Behold I thought that he would surely come to me, and stand, and call on the name of the Lord his God, and wave his hand over the place, and cure the leper. Are not Abana and Pharpar, the rivers of Damascus, better than all the waters of Israel? Could I not wash in them and be clean?" (2 Kings 5:12). So he turned and went away in a rage. The sweeping of God stirred up the dust of his anger and many have reacted in the same way. Confronted by suffering and death they think of God as a torturer and of life as a circus where men are savaged without reason, without recourse, and without the right of appeal.

Sometimes the sweepings of God stir up our anger, at

other times they stir up our fears. That was the experience of both Isaiah the prophet and Saul of Tarsus. Thus in the year that King Uzziah died, Isaiah caught a vision of God's holiness and was brought thereby to the realization of his own sinfulness. Filled with terror at the thought of falling into the hands of the Living God, he exclaims, "Woe is me! For I am lost; for I am a man of unclean lips, and I dwell in the midst of a people of unclean lips; for my eyes have seen the King, the Lord of hosts" (Isaiah 6:5). The same thing happened to Saul of Tarsus. As a Pharisee he felt that he had fulfilled all the requirements of the law. "As to righteousness under the law blameless" (Philippiasns 3:6). However, as he looked at the life of Christ, he came to see that he had fallen far short of God's glory. He awoke to the realization that he was a man under judgment and, like Robert Murray McCheyne, he cried:

When free grace awoke me by light from on high,
Then legal fears shook me—I trembled to die;
No refuge, no safety, in self could I see:
'Jehovah Tsidkenu' my Savior must be![76]

The sweepings of God stirred up the dust of his fears!

At other times the sweepings of God stir up the dust of our hopes. The Scriptures tell us that one day, as Jesus entered the city of Capernaum, a centurion came forward, beseeching Him, and saying, "Lord, do not trouble yourself, for I am not worthy to have you come under my roof; therefore I did not presume to come to you. But say the word, and let my servant be healed. For I am a man set under authority, with soldiers under me: and I say to one, 'Go,' and he goes; and to another, 'Come,' and he comes; and to my slave, 'Do this,' and he does it." When Jesus heard this He marveled at him, saying, "Not even in Israel have I found such faith" (Luke 7:6-9). The sweeping of God may have destroyed that man's confidence in the physicians of his day but it stirred up the dust of his hope in Christ. Undoubtedly he had heard of the miracles which Jesus had done and, hope rising within him, he resolved to seek Jesus out and he did!

That suggests the purpose of the sweeping. It is not without dust but it is through that sweeping that the lost coins of humanity are found. The writer of Deuteronomy makes that quite clear. He is talking about God's dealings with Israel and he says, "He [God] found him in a desert land, and in the howling waste of the wilderness; He encircled him, He cared for him, He kept him as the apple of His eye. Like an eagle that stirs up the nest, that flutters over its young, spreading out its wings, catching them, bearing them on its pinions, the Lord did lead them" (Deuteronomy 32:10-12a). The editor there is saying that the disturbance is not without purpose. Just as through this harrowing experience the eagle is teaching the eaglets to fly so through the sweeping God is seeking His lost coins.

Does that not explain the Divine disturbance of our lives? It is God's way of seeking and saving that which is lost. Namaan may have been angry at first but, listening to the counsel of his servants, he faces his need and swallows his pride, and dips himself seven times in the waters of the Jordan and "his flesh was restored like the flesh of a little child and he was clean" (2 Kings 5:1). The lost was found! Saul of Tarsus may have feared the judgment of God but that fear drove him, not to despair, but into the waiting arms of the Savior. As for the centurion, his hopes were realized for when "those who had been sent home returned to the house, they found his servant well" (Luke 7:10).[77]

The sweeping of God is not without dust. Has He been stirring up a dust in your life? Has He been arousing your wrath? Has He been raising fears within your heart? Has He been awakening hope within your soul? Then do not fear for these things are the harbingers of salvation. Therefore "look up and raise your heads, because your redemption is drawing near" (Luke 21:28).

Chapter Eight

UNTIL SHE FINDS IT

"What woman, having ten silver coins, if she loses one coin, does not light a lamp, and sweep the house, and seek diligently until she finds it?" (Luke 15:8). Jesus may have seen something like that in His own home in Nazareth. The coin had a "silver content that was worth about sixteen cents"[78] but it would be a financial disaster for a poor woman to lose it. After all, it was a day's wage for a working man[79] and, for a family man living on the edge of poverty, the absence of even that amount would be sorely missed. The loss, however, was probably sentimental as well as financial for, as indicated above in chapter six, the ten coins likely constituted the necklace or headdress which was the ancient equivalent of our wedding ring. If that was the case, the ten coins were her very own and could not be taken from her even for debt.[80] At any rate, having lost it, the woman lit a lamp and proceeded "to sweep the house and seek diligently until she found it and when she had found it, she called together her friends and neighbors, saying, 'Rejoice with me, for I have found the coin which I had lost'" (Luke 15:9).

This parable, like the parable of the lost sheep, was originally intended as an answer to the criticism of the Pharisees and Scribes that "this man receives sinners and eats with them."[81] To which Jesus responds by saying that God claims all the coins of humanity for His own. Thus one day the Pharisees came to Him saying, "Is it lawful to pay taxes to Caesar, or not?" But Jesus, aware of their malice, replied, "Why put me to the test, you hypocrites? Show me the money for the tax." They brought Him a coin. Taking it, Jesus said to them, "Whose likeness and inscription is this?" They said, "Caesar's." Whereupon He said to them, "Render unto Caesar the things that are Caesar's and to God the things that are God's" (Matthew 22:17-21). Upon the coins of the realm there was the likeness of Caesar but, as Jesus knew full well, the coins of humanity are all made "in the image of God."[82]

Lorado Taft once set up *A Statue of a Boy* by Donatello. He wanted to light it so he set some lights on the floor but, with the lights shining in the boy's face, he looked like a moron. Taft tried every arrangement he could think of but to no avail. Finally, he put the lights above the boy and let them shine down on him. Then he stood back and gazed at the statue in amazement for the boy looked like an angel.[83] That is a parable. When we look at the lost coins of humanity in the light of our earthly wisdom and our materialistic standards of success they appear to have little value. Indeed, we may feel that they are unimportant, part of the flotsam and jetsam of life, not worth bothering about. But when we look at them in the light of heaven, when we view them through the eyes of Jesus Christ, we see there the "likeness" of God and know that they belong to Him.

That is why God puts such a high valuation even upon coins that are marred and defaced. It was just a coin but, in the parable, the women of the house lit a lamp, and swept the house, and searched diligently until she found it! It is just a life, a human derelict, but God wants it for His own. Why?

Not because of the intrinsic value of the human coin, for the human body, even allowing for inflation, is worth only a paltry sum. Not because of the scarcity of the coins, for the human race constitutes a great multitude. Not because these human coins have great potentiality, for oftentimes they are so worn and effaced that they are of little use to either God or man. Nevertheless God places a high value upon them because they bear His "image," because they belong to Him, because they are His "special possession" (Exodus 19:5 N.E.B);[84] so, even though they are marred and scratched and worn, He loves them with a high and holy love (1 John 4:10).

In view of that, two things follow as naturally and inevitably as day follows night. If we bear the "image" of God and are loved of Him, we should live not as tramps and derelicts but as sons of God and as children of the King.

> I'm a child of the King,
> A child of the King:
> With Jesus my Savior,
> I'm a child of the King.[85]

And beyond that, we who profess to be followers of the Galilean should regard these lost coins of humanity, these outcasts and pariahs, not with disdain and contempt but with loving compassion and heartfelt concern. They are more than misfits and failures; they are souls for whom Christ died!

God claims all the coins of humanity as His own but sometimes these coins are caught in the fell clutch of circumstance and displaced. Thus, in the parable of the lost sheep, there was no wilfulness or disobedience. The sheep, being a sheep, simply followed its instincts. It nibbled a tuft of grass here and a tuft of grass there. It meandered from this patch of green to that patch over yonder until quite unintentionally and quite unwittingly it wandered away from the tender shepherd's care. How different was the case of the prodigal son! There was revolt there. He was irked by the restrictions of home and by the loving restraint with which his father surrounded him. So, one day, he went to his father and said, "Father, give me the share of property that falls to me." So his father gave him his portion. Not many days after he gathered all that he had and took his journey into a far country, and there he squandered his property in loose living" (Luke 15:11-14). There was rebellion there, defiance of his father's will but, in the parable of the lost coin, the coin was passive and unresisting. Loosed from its setting by wear, it was caught by the pull of gravity and fell and, being round, rolled into some dark corner or crevice. As Alexander Maclaren puts it, "The coin was heavy so it fell; it was round so it rolled; it was dead, so it lay."[86] There are people like that. They are caught in the grip of circumstance and imprisoned. They can't make a living so they steal. Brought up in sordid surroundings, they drink. Discriminated against, they are driven by fear. That is the point of Richard Wright's *Native Son*. Driven by fear Biggar Thomas kills a white girl and then, pursued by the law, sinks deeper and deeper into crime until eventually he is captured, tried and executed.[87]

When that happens we are quick to condemn but, on the day of judgment, the Judge may well point His finger of condemnation, not at the lost coin but at us, for allowing such conditions to exist for we are our brother's keeper and are responsible for him. That is a heavy responsibility but it helps to realize that in the search for these lost coins we are not alone; God is searching too! After all, He is not only God in heaven, He is also God here upon the earth where He seeks men out and encounters them in such a way that "the natural becomes the transparency of the divine."[88] Then, quickened by the Holy Spirit, men recognize His presence and grasp His words to their souls.[89] Sometimes that revelation is mediated through nature—in a vision of the night (Genesis 15:1), through the lips of messengers (Genesis 18:1-2), or by means of "a bush that burns but is not consumed" (Exodus 3:2). At other times is takes place through a "cumulative process of events and their interpretation in history."[90] Such was the history of Israel as seen in the migration of the patriarchs, in Israel's deliverance from Egyptian bondage, in their settlement in the land of Canaan, in the kingship of David and Solomon, in the ministry of the great prophets, in the tragedy of the Babylonian captivity and in Israel's return from it, and in the rebuilding of the nation around the second temple. The climax to that whole process of revelation, however, was the coming of Christ "to seek and to save that which was lost" (Luke 19:10); for, as men stood in His presence, they were constrained to acknowledge Him as Lord, a confession which actually was made by Peter (Luke 5:8), and Thomas (John 20:28), and Paul (Acts 9:4).

That can mean only one thing. God has been searching for His lost coins and, according to Jesus, He will not abandon the search until He finds them. In other words, the search did not end with the resurrection of Christ, with the proclamation of salvation and new life available in Him. It still goes on! But to what avail if we refuse to respond? Surely we should recognize the alternative and remember the words of Simon Peter, "To whom shall we go? You have the words of eternal life!" (John 6:68).

Part Three

THE PARABLE OF THE LOST BOY

There was a man who had two sons; and the younger of them said to his father, "Father, give me the share of property that falls to me." And he divided his living between them. Not many days later, the younger son gathered all he had and took his journey into a far country, and there he squandered his property in loose living. And when he had spent everything a great famine arose in that country, and he began to be in want. So he went and joined himself to one of the citizens of that country, who sent him into his fields to feed swine. And he would gladly have fed on the pods that the swine ate; and no one gave him anything. But when he came to himself he said, "How many of my father's hired servants have bread enough and to spare, but I perish here with hunger! I will arise and go to my father, and I will say to him, Father, I have sinned against heaven and before you; I am no longer worthy to be called your son; treat me as one of your hired servants." And he rose and came to his father. But while he was yet at a distance, his father saw him and had compassion, and ran and embraced him and kissed him. And he said to him, "Father, I have sinned against heaven and before you; I am no longer worthy to be called your son." But the father said to his servants, "Bring quickly the best robe, and put it on him; and put a ring on his hand, and shoes on his feet; and bring the fatted calf and kill it, and let us eat and be merry; for this my son was dead and is alive again; he was lost and is found." And they began to be merry.

Luke 15: 11-24

Chapter Nine

THE BEST STORY IN THE WORLD

Lindsay Gregg tells of an interesting experience he had with the story of the prodigal son. He was taking a long train ride and needed something to read. On the newsstand he found a small volume entitled *The World's Best Stories*. "I love good stories," he said, "so I bought the book." Comfortably seated in the train he glanced over the table of contents and was surprised to learn that the title of the fourth story was "The Prodigal Son," by Jesus. "There and then," he says, "I decided to make an experiment. I would start with the first story of the book and read straight through to the story of the prodigal son and, being as fair minded and impartial as possible, I would try to evaluate it. It took me two hours to read the first three stories. Then I turned to " The Prodigal Son" but, before I finished reading it, the tears were coursing down my cheeks and when I came to the end I said a reverent 'Amen! It's the best story in the world!'"[91]

There are good reasons for that appraisal. To begin with, the parable of the prodigal son is the best story in the world because it deals with the best of all subjects. Helmut Thielicke, whose preaching filled the chapel of the University of Hamburg Sunday after Sunday with some three thousand worshipers, tells how several years ago he set his little son down in front of a large mirror. At first the little lad did not recognize himself because he was too young but he obviously enjoyed seeing the small image that smiled at him from the glass wall. Then, all of a sudden, the expression on his face changed as he began to recognize the similarity between the motions he made and those which he saw in the mirror . . . . He seemed to be saying, "That's me."[92]

That is what happens when we read this story of the prodigal son. We discover that Jesus is talking about us, about each and everyone of us. Thus the parable talks about our home. It speaks of our Heavenly Father and of His love for us and about the splendor and comfort of the dwelling place which He has given us here upon the earth.

My Father is rich in houses and lands,
He holdeth the wealth of the world in His hands.
Of rubies and diamonds, of silver and gold,
His coffers are full, He has riches untold.[93]

The parable refers to the endowment which we have all received, to the portion of goods that has fallen to us, to the healthy bodies and keen minds and strong wills which God has given us and it reminds us of the peace and serenity of our childhood days.

Then the parable talks about our leaving that home, for the prodigal is not only the adulterer and the murderer, not only the liar and the thief, he is everyone of us. The prodigal is anyone who has set his will against the will of God and that means each and everyone of us for "we have all sinned and come short of the glory of God" (Romans 3:23). "All we like sheep have gone astray, we have turned everyone to his own way" (Isaiah 53:6). We are not only those who have fallen short of God's glory, but we are also those who have rebelled against His authority and ignored His commands. "There was a man who had two sons; and the younger of them said to his father, 'Father, give me the share of property that falls to me!' And he divided his living between them. Not many days later, the younger son gathered all he had and took his journey into a far country, and there he squandered his property in loose living" (Luke 15:11-13). That is not only the story of the prodigal, that is also an account of your departure and mine from the Father's house.

Nor is that all. The parable talks about our home, and about our departure from the Father's house, and it talks about our homesickness. "And when he had spent everything, a great famine arose in that country and he began to be in want. So he went and joined himself to one of the citizens of that country who sent him into his fields to feed swine; and no man gave him anything"(Luke 15:14-16). It is the Master's way of saying that we are made for fellowship with God and that we can never be permanently satisfied with the things of this world, with the mere stimulation of our senses, with material things, with the husks which the swine do eat! "As a hart longs for flowing streams, so longs my soul for Thee, O God. My soul thirsts for God, for the Living God. When shall I come and behold the face of God" (Psalm 42:1-2). The blank in the human heart is "a God shaped blank"![94]

This story of the prodigal son is the best story in the world because it deals with the best of all subjects—it talks about men and women, it speaks about you and me—and it is the best of all stories because it tells about the best of all decisions—the decision "to seek the Lord while He may be found and to call upon Him while He is near" (Isaiah 55:6). It lets us know when the prodigal made his decision. It was when "he came to himself" (Luke 15:17), when he realized how foolish he had been, when he discovered that sinning is a scattering business, that it does not satisfy the hunger of the soul and that there is no future to it. It explains why he made that decision—not only because he had come to the end of his resources—"he spent all and began to be in want" (Luke 15:14)—but also because he remembered the Father's house and the carefree days of innocence and youth and "the bread enough and to spare" (Luke 15:17). And it tells us what he said when he returned.

André Gide, the French writer, has his own ending to the parable. He has the prodigal send his older brother off to the far country so that he, in turn, can grow up and mature.[95] His idea is that it was good for the younger brother to be lost for a time, beneficial for him to sin so that he could experience the realities of life and so really appreciate the comforts of home. The prodigal says nothing about that; he knew better. He knew from his own experience that sin does not develop. It destroys. It does not mature; it mixes up our lives. It leaves scars and remorse. So what the prodigal actually said to himself and then to his father was, "I will arise and go to my father and I will say to him, 'Father, I have sinned against heaven and before you; I am no longer worthy to be called your son; treat me as one of your hired servants'" (Luke 15:18-19).

This parable of the lost boy is the best of all stories, not only because it deals with the best of all subjects and because it tells about the best of all decisions, but also because it has the best of all endings. There could have been other endings to the story. The prodigal might never have come back. He might have been swallowed up in the far country and never been heard from again. Or, he might have come back too late. He might have come back to find his father dead and the opportunity for forgiveness gone forever. That was the story of Charlie Grant in Ian Maclaren's *The Days of Auld Lang Syne.* Charlie came back to Drumtochty and made his way to the cemetery where he found the stone bearing the names of his mother and grandmother. Then, says Ian Maclaren, "he knelt on the turf and, taking off his hat, prayed God that his sin might be forgiven, and that one day he might meet the trusting hearts that had not despaired of his return."[96]

There could have been other endings to the parable but Jesus, knowing the greatness of God's heart and the wonder of His love, gave it the best of all endings. The prodigal came back to find his father waiting and watching. He came back to God's forgiveness and pardon. He came back to the father's bounty. "Bring forth the best robe and put it on him and put a ring on his hand and shoes on his feet" (Luke 15:22). And he came back to the father's joy. "Bring the fatted calf and kill it, and let us eat and be merry; for this my son was dead and is alive again; he was lost and is found" (Luke 15:23-4).

That is the best of all endings because it is God's truth. It is the word of the Gospel. In *The Sky Pilot,* Ralph Connor tells of a young man who left a good home in Scotland to work on one of the ranches in western Canada. One day, as the "Pilot" was making his rounds and going from shack to shack, he heard someone singing the twenty-third Psalm. He went to the house from whence the sound was coming and there he found a young man who was dying. The lad had been brought up in a Christian home but now he lay dying an early death because of sins which he had committed. The "Pilot" spoke tenderly to him and before he left was asked to read a letter which had come that very day from the lad's mother. He read it and the letter closed something like this. "And, oh, Davie, laddie, if ever your heart turns home again, remember the door is aye open, and it's joy you'll bring with you to us all."[97]

That is the best of all endings to the story of life. Like the prodigal we can come home, not because we are worthy—for we are not—but because God's love is so full and free. "For God so loved the world that He gave His only Son, that whoever believes in Him should not perish but have eternal life!" (John 3:16).

Chapter Ten

A GRAND OLD MAN

The story is told of a country lad who listened in an English cathedral to the reading of the prodigal son. Came the words, "But while he was yet at a distance, his father saw him, and had compassion and ran[98] and embraced him and kissed him" (Luke 15:20). Whereupon the lad, quite forgetful of both the place and the people, exclaimed, "Eh, but yon is a grand old man!"[99] The young man was thinking of "the father" as an earthly father and we would all agree with him, but when we realize that the father in Luke 15 is meant to portray God this parable becomes a revelation to our souls.[100] It is to that portrait of "the heavenly Father" that we now turn.

Before doing so, however, there are two observations that need to be made. The first is that this portrait of God is the real theme of the parable.[101] It is not primarily a story about the prodigal son, or about the far country, or about the elder brother. It is a story about God. Thus the parable begins by pointing to Him—"There was a man" (Luke 15:11)—and it ends with the words of the Father—"And he said to him, 'Son, you are always with me, and all that is mine is thine. It was fitting to make merry and be glad, for this my son was dead, and is alive again; he was lost and is found'" (Luke 15:31-2). This portrait of the Father is the real theme of the parable and it stands in sharp contrast to the idea of

God which many people had in Jesus' day. They thought of Him as a great God, as the mighty God, as the Lord God Omnipotent. Indeed they could have sung with real fervor and conviction the familiar words of Stuart Hine's hymn—

> O Lord my God! When I in awesome wonder
> Consider all the *worlds Thy hands have made,
> I see the stars, I hear the *rolling thunder,
> Thy power throughout the universe displayed
> Then sings my soul, my Savior God to Thee:
> How great Thou art! How great Thou art![102]
>> *Author's original words were *works* and *mighty.*

In the days of our Lord people thought of God as a great God and as a holy God. To them it was "a fearful thing to fall into the hands of the living God" (Hebrews 10:31), for "Thou" they said, "Thou art of purer eyes than to behold evil and canst not look on wrong" (Habakkuk 1:13). To them God was a God of justice who gave to every man his just deserts. They thought of Him as a great God, as a holy God and as a distant God—one who was transcendent, far distant in the heavens. Thus Solomon prayed that God would hear from "heaven His dwelling place" and that when He heard He would forgive (1 Kings 8:30).

Our parable does not repudiate those descriptions of God for they contain much truth, but it does point to some aspects of God's character which, until then, had been largely overlooked. Some aspects which make us exclaim with the English lad, "Eh, but yon is a grand old man!" What are they?

The first is the father's wisdom, his wise handling of his boy. "And he said, 'There was a certain man who had two sons: and the younger of them said to his father, "Father give me the share of property that falls to me." And he divided his living between them'" (Luke 15:11-12). Oftentimes we associate the role of a father with that of a martinet. We think of him as a disciplinarian. There is obvious truth there for fathers are meant to exercise discipline. Indeed, in the Scriptures, they are urged not to spare the rod lest they spoil the child (Proverbs 24:6).[103]

Fathers should bring their children up and not be brought up by them. Nevertheless, there comes a time when children can no longer be forced to do things. There comes a time in their lives when they must make their own decisions and stand on their own feet and choose whose authority they will recognize. It is the acceptance of this reality which underlies the father's wise handling of his boy. When the lad came to him saying, "Father, give me the share of property that falls to me" (Luke 15:12), he let him go. "He divided his living between them" (Luke 15:12b). He made no attempt to restrain him or prevent him from going. He let the boy go, hoping that eventually he would "come to himself" (Luke 15:17), that he would realize how foolish he had been and would come home of his own volition.

In the parable that picture of the father is a picture of God. He is a wise Father. He wants sons not slaves. He wants us to serve Him of our own free will so He refuses to coerce us. He gives us freedom of choice. He lets us go our own way and He waits patiently for our return for He knows that those who come back freely and without compulsion make good sons and daughters. He is a wise God. Ian Maclaren makes that quite clear when he sets the wondrous ways of God over against our poor, bungling human methods.

Thus when Marget Howe went to see Lacklan Campbell to console him over the loss of his daughter who had run away to London, Lacklan refused to talk. "She is not anything to me this day," he said. "See, I will show you what I have done, for she has been a black shame to my name." He opened his Bible and there was Flora's name, scored out.

When Marget saw that she opened the dykes and allowed the flood of her wrath to pour out. "This is what you have done," she said, "and you let a woman see your work. You are an old man, and in sore travail, but I tell you before God you have the greater shame. Just twenty years of age this spring and her mother dead. No woman to watch over her, and she wandered from the fold, and all you can do is to take her name out of your Bible. Woe is me if our Father had blotted out our names from the Book of Life when we left His house. But He sent His son to seek us, and a weary road He came."[104] How wisely God handles us all. Surely we can trust wisdom like that!

Another side of the father's character which the parable brings out is his love, for there we see the extent of his provision for his son. Sometimes we don't realize the measure of our parents' sacrifice for us until we get away from home and have to provide for ourselves and for others. As children we take it for granted that there will be food on the table, and clothes for us to wear, and a home to live in and, as we grow older, that the car will be available whenever we want it. But when we leave home, when we have to provide those things ourselves, we begin to realize how much our parents must have loved us and how much they must have given up on our behalf. That realization came home to the prodigal in the far country. "But, when he came to himself, he said, 'How many of my father's hired servants have bread enough and to spare but I perish here with hunger'" (Luke 15:17). It was then that he grasped something of his father's love and the fulness of His bounty.

If that can be said of our earthly fathers it applies even more to our Father in heaven. Thinking of His provision for our needs one is reminded of Marget sitting in the garden with her son Gordie. They are talking about the days when he was young and when he had awakened in the middle of the night, fearful of God's wrath and judgment. When she asked him if he remembered that night, he replied, "Ay, and you kissed me, mother, and you said, 'Am I a good mother to you?' And when I could do nothing but hold on to you, you said, 'Be sure God must be a hantle kinder.'"[105]

God must be a lot kinder! That is the picture of God given to us in this immortal story and it is true. Think of God's provision for our material needs—His forethought in creation, His making the sun to shine and the rain to fall so that we might have food. His hand resting upon us in protection and blessing. Consider what He has given us for our social welfare—He has taken us as individuals and set us in families, and He has given us the fellowship of "kindred minds which is like to that above."[106] Nor is that all; He has provided for our spiritual needs—He sent His Son into the world to be our Savior, "to bear our sins in His own body on the tree" (1 Peter 2:24), "to die the just for the unjust, that He might bring us to God" (1 Peter 3:18), and "that we might go at last to heaven, saved by His precious blood."[107] Our God is a good God. He is a "hantle kinder," a whole lot kinder than ever the best of human fathers!

Yes, and He is a God of grace. That is something which this story of the prodigal son also emphasizes because it tells us of the warm welcome which the prodigal received when he returned home. He deserved nothing. He had been given his inheritance and had "squandered his property in loose living" (Luke 15:13). He had "devoured his living with harlots" (Luke 15:30).

In truth he was "no longer worthy to be called his father's son" (Luke 15:19), but, when he tried to make confession, to declare this, his father cut him short saying, "Bring forth the best robe, and put it on him; and put a ring on his hand, and shoes on his feet; and bring hither the fatted calf and kill it, and let us eat and be merry" (Luke 15:22-23). The best robe was reserved for distinguished guests.[108] A ring on the hand was a symbol of authority.[109] Shoes were the mark of a son and heir—only slaves went barefoot.[110] And the "fatted calf," taken early from the mother cow, was kept for special occasions.[111] Everything speaks of the warmth and genuineness of the father's welcome.

That should make clear to us the wonder of God's "incomprehensible grace,"[112] for this parable tells us that God's favor does not depend upon our worthiness but that it is a "bubbling spring,"[113] a *quellende liebe,*[114] which flows of its own accord from His heart to ours. It assures us that God wants us to come "home," that He stands ready to cover the marks of the Far Country, and that He has a place for us at His table. It proclaims the good news that God is not only willing to forgive but also to forget. That He promises to cast our sins into the sea of His forgetfulness. That He stands ready to put them behind His back.

Our God is not only a wise God, and a loving God, He is also a God of grace, a God of amazing grace! Dostoievsky, the famous Russian novelist, was convinced of that. When he lay dying he called the members of his family into the room and had them read this parable of the prodigal son. He listened with his eyes closed, absorbed in thought. Then he spoke. "My children," he said in his feeble voice, "never forget what you have just heard. Have absolute faith in God and never despair of His pardon. I love you dearly but my love is nothing compared to the love of God. Even if you should be so unhappy as to commit some dreadful crime, never despair of God. You are His children; humble yourselves before Him, as before your father; implore His pardon and He will rejoice over your repentance, as the father rejoiced over that of the prodigal son!"[115] That is the God we worship, a God of wondrous mercy and amazing grace!

Our English friend is right. "Yon is a grand old man!" Then let us leave the Far Country and set out for the Father's house.

Come home! Come home
Ye who are weary, come home!
Earnestly, tenderly, Jesus is calling—
Calling, O sinner, 'Come home!'[116]

Chapter Eleven

THE FAR COUNTRY

Where is the far country? It is on no map and it can be located on no continent. It has been customary however, following the lead of our parable, to locate it in the land of passion. "But when this son of yours came, who has devoured your living with harlots, you killed for him the fatted calf!" (Luke 15:30). Thus in popular thought the prodigal is always immoral and the far country is usually the land of undisciplined sexual passion. So when we think of prodigals we think not only of the younger son but of Gomer, the wife of Hosea, who left her husband to seek for other lovers; we think of Mary of Magdala who was a woman of the streets; or we think of Sonya, who was part of the flotsam and jetsam of the city's wreckage in Dostoievsky's great book, *Crime And Punishment.* That is natural because you often find prodigals in the land of passion. "Not many days later, the younger son gathered all he had and took his journey into a far country, and there he squandered his property in loose living" (Luke 15:13).

The far country is often the land of passion but it is more than that. It is also the land of indulgence. One thinks of that scene in Dickens's *Tale of Two Cities* where Sydney Carton is captivated by the beauty and personality of Lucie Manette. He sees himself aspiring to her hand, his life characterized by honorable ambition, self-denial and perseverance but the vision lasts only for a moment. He climbs the stairs to his chamber, throws himself down in his clothes upon the neglected bed, and weeps until his pillow is wet with wasted tears. Commenting on it Dickens writes: "Sadly, sadly the sun rose; and it rose upon no sadder sight than the man of good capabilities, and good emotions, incapable of their directed exercise, incapable of his own help and his own happiness, sensible of the blight on him, and resigning himself to let it eat him away."[117] It is the picture of a prodigal, there is no doubt about that, but for him the far country was not the land of passion but the land of indulgence. Sydney Carton could not control his thirst for alcohol and the same thing has been true of many prodigals who have come to grief in that country.

For some prodigals the far country is the land of passion, for others it is the land of indulgence, and for still others it is the land of worldliness. That is the country where more prodigals come to grief than in any other place. It is the land where the elder brother was lost. He was never immoral, he probably never drank to excess, but he was lost nonetheless—he lost his relationship with his father, and his love for his brother, in making money and getting ahead, and climbing the social ladder. Certainly all prodigals aren't penurious—you will see them in their evening clothes, and their expensive cars, and their plush offices—but they are lost nonetheless, lost in the land of worldliness!

Where then is the far country? It is not any one of those countries that have been mentioned but in all of them. It is, as Dr. Ellis Fuller once put it, "It is anywhere that a man tries to live without God."[118]

That brings us to a second question. Why do people go into the far country? Why do they do anything? Usually they have more than one reason and the same thing is true of those who "gather all they have and take their journey into a far country" (Luke 15:13).

Sometimes they go because they are offended by the restraints and restrictions of the father's house. Fathers are older than sons and presumably know more about life, more about the pitfalls and dangers that are there. That is why there are rules and regulations in the father's house. It isn't that fathers want to deprive their sons of their legitimate freedom but because they want to ensure that freedom. Prodigals don't always realize that and sometimes they are irked by their father's decisions and in high dudgeon set off for the far country. That is why, in the parable of the prodigal son, the younger brother left. He wanted his own way. He wanted to be free. So he rebelled against discipline and he scorned advice.

> My father glooms and advises me,
> And Mother catechizes me,
> 'Til I want to go out and swear.[119]

Sometimes prodigals go into the far country because they are offended by the restraints and restrictions of the father's house. At other times they go because they are drawn by the sights and sounds of that land. The bright lights are appealing and the music is exciting and there is a glamour and a fascination about it all. No one who has any acquaintance with the world will deny that. The tragedy, however, is that the world has been oversold. It can't live up to its billing. It can't give what it promises. It simply cannot satisfy the hunger of the human heart. That is something which many a prodigal has discovered to his regret, too late. They leave home and go off to the far country because it appears to be everything that they want only to find through bitter experience that appearances are deceiving and that their expectations are unfulfilled.

Still others are driven out of their fathers' homes by their elder brothers.[120] Rudyard Kipling has a poem called *The Prodigal Son* {Western Version}, in which he makes the prodigal say:

> I was never very refined, you see,
> (And it weighs on my brother's mind do you see),
> But there's no reproach among swine do you see,
> For being a bit of a swine.

> So I'm off with wallet and staff to eat
> The bread that is three parts chaff to wheat,
> But glory be! there's a laugh to it,
> Which isn't the case when we dine.

> I'm leaving, Pater, Good-bye to you!
> God bless you, Mater! I'll write to you . . .
> I wouldn't be impolite to you,
> But, Brother, you are a hound![121]

Sad to say, sometimes prodigals go into the far country because of their elder brothers, because of their lack of love, and their refusal to forgive, and their self-righteousness, and because they refuse to let younger brothers take their proper place in the family circle.

That is always a tragedy for the far country marks a man and he can never be the same again for once a thing is done it can never be undone. An incident in the life of Lou Gehrig, the New York baseball player, illustrates that. Here is the way a sports writer for a New York paper described what happened. "Lou Gehrig came to bat with two out in the ninth inning. The winning runs were on second and third. The count on Lou Gehrig went to three balls and two strikes. The grandstands were in an uproar. The pitcher wound up deliberately and the third strike came smoking in right over the middle of the plate and the umpire called, 'Strike,' for Lou Gehrig hadn't moved his bat. Very slowly Lou turned and spoke to the umpire. At that, the crowd went wild for no one had ever heard Lou Gehrig argue with an umpire.

"We reporters all piled over the seats and right out onto the field. We swarmed around the umpire. 'What did Lou Gehrig say to you?' we all asked in one breath. The umpire smiled and yelled to Lou Gehrig to come over. 'Lou,' he said, 'tell the boys what you said to me when I called that third strike on you.' 'Ump, I only said that I would give ten dollars to have that one back!'"[122] Of course he couldn't have it back for ten dollars, or for a hundred dollars, or even for a thousand and it is the same with life. The prodigal who goes into the far country can never be what he might have been had he stayed at home.

The marks of the far country may be covered so that they are not seen by everyone but they are there nonetheless as prodigals themselves admit:

Yes, Thou forgivest, but with all forgiving
Cans't not renew mine innocence again.[123]

Regardless of why they leave home, the going of the prodigal into the far country is always a tragedy!

That tragedy compels us to ask whether there is any way back from the far country?   Yes, but it is a hard road to travel for it is always hard for a man to face himself, to admit that he made a mistake and to actually set out for the father's house. It is difficult to say, "I have sinned against heaven and before you; I am no longer worthy to be called your son" (Luke 15:18-9), but it is even more difficult "to arise and come."

You see that in the story of Raskolnikov, the worst of prodigal sons as portrayed by Dostoievsky in *Crime and Punishment*.   Raskolnikov murdered both Alyona and Lizavesta and he carried the burden of that crime upon his soul for many a day. Eventually the burden became too much for him and he decided to take the way back from the far country but it was hard. He went to the police station, pale and distraught, but could say nothing so he left again.

The second time he did better. "Raskolnikov, with white lips and staring eyes, came slowly nearer. He walked right to the table, leaned his hand on it, tried to say something but could not; only incoherent sounds were audible. 'You are feeling ill, a chair!   Here, sit down!   Some water!' Raskolnikov dropped on to a chair but kept his eyes fixed on the face of Ilya Petrovitch which expressed unpleasant surprise. Both looked at one another for a minute and waited. Water was brought. 'It was I . . . ,' began Raskolnikov. 'Drink some water.' Raskolnikov refused the water with his hand and softly and brokenly but distinctly said, 'It was I who killed the old pawnbroker woman and her sister Lizavesta with an axe and robbed them.'"[124] The way back from the far country is a hard way.

Yes, and it is a long way back. In returning to the father's house a man oftentimes has to fight a battle with himself and his evil habits and that takes not only God, and effort on our part, but time. That is the essence of Ralph Connor's story about Gwen. She was a wild, wilful young thing, living with her father in the foothills of the Rockies. One day she was thrown from her horse and was told by the Doctor that she would never walk, or ride again. It was then that the "Sky Pilot" told her the story of the canyon.

He told how, at first, there were no canyons, but only the broad, open prairie. Then the Master of the Prairie, walking over his great lawns where only grass grew, asked the Prairie, "Where are your flowers?" To which the Prairie replied, "Master, I have no seeds." So the Master spoke to the birds and they carried seeds of every kind of flower and strewed them far and wide so that soon the Prairie bloomed with crocuses and roses and buffalo beans and the yellow crowfoot and the wild sunflowers and the red lilies all summer long.

The Master was pleased but He missed the flowers He loved best, and He said to the Prairie, "Where are the clematis, the columbine, the sweet violets and wind flowers, and all the ferns and flowering shrubs?" So again the Master spoke to the birds and again they carried the seeds and strewed them far and wide.

But again, when the Master came He could not find the flowers He loved best of all, and He said, "Where are those, my sweetest flowers?"And the Prairie cried sorrowfully, "Oh Master, I cannot keep the flowers, for the winds sweep fiercely, and the sun beats upon my breast and they wither up and fly away."

Then the Master spoke to the Lightning, and with one swift blow the Lightning cleft the Prairie to the heart. And the Prairie rocked and groaned in agony, and for many a day moaned bitterly over its black, jagged, gaping wound. But the Little Swan poured its waters through the cleft, and carried down deep black mold, and once more the birds carried seeds and strewed them in the canyon. And after a long time the rough rocks were decked out with soft mosses and trailing vines, and all the nooks were hung with clematis and columbine, and great elms lifted their huge tops high up into the sunlight, and down about their feet clustered the low cedars and balsams, and everywhere the violets and wind-flower and maiden-hair grew and bloomed, till the canyon became the Master's place for rest and peace and joy.

The quaint tale ended, Gwen lay quiet for some moments and then she said wistfully, "There are no flowers in my canyon, but only ragged rocks." To which the "Sky Pilot" responded, "Some day they will bloom, Gwen dear; He will find them, and we, too, shall see them."[125] And they did for in time Gwen's room became the brightest spot in the house!

The way back from the far country may be a hard way back, and a long way back, but it is also a glad way back. It is worth coming back because at the end of the journey there is the father's welcome, and the father's forgiveness, and the father's house. "But while he was yet at a distance, his father saw him, and had compassion, and ran and embraced him and kissed him" (Luke 15:20). That homecoming brings to mind the night Flora Campbell came home. Speaking of it afterwards Flora said to Marget Howe. "It is a pity you have no Gaelic. It is the best of all languages for loving. There are fifty words for *darling*, and my father will be calling me every one that night I came home."[126] That makes it a glad way back and that can be the joyful end of the journey for us all!

Chapter Twelve

WHEN HE CAME TO HIMSELF

A wag has pointed to the distress of the prodigal by suggesting that as things became difficult he began to pawn his clothes. First he pawned his coat, then he pawned his shirt, and finally "he came to himself" (Luke 15:17). It is a great day in a man's life when he makes that discovery, not when he finds that he has a body but "when he comes to himself," when he takes stock of himself and his situation and his future. It is of such an experience that these words of our parable speak.

Thus when it tells us that the prodigal "came to himself" it means that he discovered who he was. One day Arthur Schopenhauer was walking down the street when he accidentally bumped into a stranger. The stranger, upset by what had happened, turned on the philosopher and exclaimed, "Who are you anyway?" To which Schopenhauer, lost in meditation, answered, "Who am I? How I wish I knew!"[127] It is a question we all need to ask ourselves and there in the far country the prodigal found the answer that he was looking for.

It is significant that the prodigal found the answer in

the far country "when he had spent everything . . . and began to be in want" (Luke 15:14). When our health is good, when we have friends and money, we are often too busy to take stock, too preoccupied with other things to sit down and face the ultimate issues of life. But when things do not turn out as we had expected, when we are left alone and when we come to the end of our resources, we begin to ask questions. Indeed sometimes, in the providence of God, disappointment and frustration and adversity prove to be blessings in disguise.

Helmut Thielicke tells of such an instance. During World War II, in spite of Nazi opposition, he continued to give lectures on the Christian Faith. After one air raid he was helping with the clean-up operations and was standing on the edge of a huge crater opened up by an aerial bomb. "Suddenly," he says, "a woman came up to me—she was the wife of an officer who had been killed—and asked if I was Helmut Thielicke for I was covered with dust and grime and she did not recognize me at first. When I confirmed my identity she showed me her husband's cap and said, 'This is all that was left of him. Only last Thursday I was with him, attending your lecture. And now I want to thank you for preparing him for his death.'"

In commenting on that experience Thielicke added these words, "What we were doing there was teaching theology in the face of death. There the only thing that was of any help at all was the gospel itself. Everything else simply dissolved into thin air. We were living only upon the substance of our faith. And those desperate hours helped us to find that substance."[128]

The same thing happened to the prodigal. There in the

far country, where he was at the end of his resources, "he came to himself" (Luke 15:17) and discovered who he was.

What did he discover? He discovered that he was his father's son. He came to the realization that he was not made for the far country, that the constant search for excitement and thrills was an exhausting business. He awoke to the fact that the food which the swine did eat was not satisfying to him. He learned that it was not enough to have a full stomach. He yearned for something higher and better and he knew then that "there's no place like home."[129]

That is a great discovery for any man to make. In one of Eugene O'Neill's plays the central figure, a man by the name of Brown, lies dead on the street. A policeman bends over the body and asks, "What his name?" To which someone replies, "Man." Then the policeman, with notebook and pencil in hand, demands, "How do you spell it?"[130]

That is the question we all have to answer. How do you spell *man*? Who are we? The answer of the younger son as he set out for the far country was that man is an animal. All he needs is a full belly and the constant stimulation of his senses. The response of the elder brother is that man is a machine and that all he needs is work, something to do. "Lo, these many years I have served you, and I never disobeyed your command" (Luke 15:29). Not satisfied with either of those answers, the father insists that man is made "in the image of God" (Genesis 1:26), and that he is made for fellowship with God (1 John 1:3). The father is right! The prodigal "came to himself" (Luke 15:17). He discovered who he was—not an animal, nor a machine, but a son of God (1 John 3:2). It is a discovery we all need to make!

"But when he came to himself he said, 'How many of my father's hired servants have bread enough and to spare, but I perish with hunger" (Luke 15:17). If that means that the prodigal discovered who he was it also means that he came to the realization of what he had done. He came to see how foolish he had been, how irrationally he had acted.

What had he done? He had "squandered his property in loose living."[131] He had dissipated what his father had gathered through long and laborious years. He had shown himself to be an unfaithful steward. Worse than that, "he had devoured his living with harlots" (Luke 15:30). When we think of the prodigal we usually think only of the harm he did himself but we must also consider the harm and injury that he did to his companions in sin.

In one of his books George Macdonald relates a confidential conversation between two of the characters: "Do you know, Wilfrid," says one, "I once shot a little bird, for no good, but just to shoot at something. It wasn't that I didn't think of it—don't say that. I did think of it. I knew it was wrong. When I leveled my gun I thought of it quite plainly, yet I drew the trigger. It dropped, a heap of ruffled feathers. I shall never get that little bird out of my head. And the worst of it is that to all eternity I can never make any atonement." "But God will forgive you, Charley!" "What do I care for that," Wilfrid answers almost fiercely, "when the little bird cannot forgive me."[132] That is something to consider when you call to mind what the prodigal did. He injured others and that injury can never be recalled. It is the realization of that which gives point to Stopford Brooks crude but telling rhyme—

Three men went out one summer night;
No care had they, or aim;
They dined, and drank; ere we go home
We'll have, they said, a game.

Three girls began that summer night
A life of endless shame,
And went through drink, disease, and death,
As swift as raging flame.

Lawless and homeless, foul, they died;
Rich, loved and praised the men;
But when they all shall meet with God,
And justice speaks—what then?[133]

What did the prodigal do? He wasted his substance in riotous living and he left home. He brought his father grief and anguish. There have been those who criticize this parable on the ground that there is no Calvary in it. There is no cross. "Why," they say, "it is just not true that God can forgive the prodigal when he comes back from the Far Country." There is insight there. Forgiveness is costly but is there no cross in the story? Is there no Calvary there? If you think there is not stand near the father's watchtower and see him as he looks for the prodigal's return until his eyes grow dim and weary. If you think there is no Calvary there stand by the door of the father's chamber and listen as he pours out his heart in prayer and as he wets his pillow with his tears. If you think there is no Calvary there watch as the father's hair turns to silver, as the spring goes out of his step, and as his shoulders bow beneath the weight of his sorrow. There is a cross in the parable, an invisible cross. It is a cross in the father's heart! And that too, you must place at the prodigal's door.

When the prodigal "came to himself" (Luke 15:17), he discovered both who he was and what he had done. Have we? That picture of the suffering father is no myth. It is a picture of what we do to God when we spurn His love and refuse His offer of forgiveness. The New Testament offers us at least one glimpse of that suffering love when it portrays Jesus weeping over the city of Jerusalem and crying, "O Jerusalem, Jerusalem, killing the prophets and stoning those who were sent to you! How often would I have gathered your children together as a hen gathers her brood under her wings, and you would not!" (Matthew 23:37). It is that last plaintive statement which grabs our attention for if God is love we should flee to Him not from Him.

That was the insight given to the prodigal for in coming to himself he also came to a conviction as to what he should do. What was that? He realized that he should go home. It takes a real man to do that, to admit that he was wrong, that he made a mistake, that he was weak and sinful. It takes a real man to acknowledge his inability to live the kind of life he should live and to seek God's grace, and it takes a real man to persevere in the fight for righteousness and truth and love. Yet that is what the prodigal did. He went out boasting that he was the one liberated member of his family but he came back saying, "I am no longer worthy to be called your son" (Luke 15:19). He came to his father saying, "Give me the share of property that falls to me" (Luke 15:12), but he returned praying, "Treat me as one of your hired servants" (Luke 15:19). He went to the far country but, in the end, he chose the father's house. "And he arose and came to his father" (Luke 15:20).

That is what God wants of us all. He knows that we cannot remove the marks of the Far Country so He has provided for us a covering, a robe of righteousness (Isaiah 61:10). He realizes that we are weak and hungry so He provides food from heaven (John 6:31-35). Aware that we have forfeited our sonship and wasted our living, He offers to take us once more into the family circle and to seal that relationship with a ring of grace (Ephesians 1:7). All that God knows and all that God has done. And all he asks of us is that we come home!

Let me tell you a little more about Flora Campbell's homecoming. There, in London, she was sick and lonely so, hearing singing, she slipped into the shadow of a church and wept. As she did so the vision of her father's house came to her so she went on into the sanctuary. The congregation was singing—

> There is a fountain filled with blood
> Drawn from Immanuel's veins;
> And sinners, plunged beneath that flood,
> Lose all their guilty stains.[134]

The sermon that followed was on the prodigal son but there was one phrase that Flora remembered, "You are missed." "You are not forgotten or cast off," the preacher said, "you are missed." And he came back to it again and again. After the service Flora went out into the darkness, crying to herself, "Father, Father," but feeling that she could not go back. Then it occurred to her that there might be a sign and she went to her room and there was a letter and this is what it said. "Your father loves you more than ever!" And she said, "This is my warrant!"[135] So she came home!

This parable is our warrant and with that warrant in our hands let us leave the Far Country and hasten to the Father's house. "But while he was yet at a distance, his father saw him and had compassion, and ran and embraced him and kissed him. . . . And the father said to his servants, 'Bring quickly the best robe, and put it on him; and put a ring on his hand, and shoes on his feet; and bring the fatted calf and kill it, and let us eat and be merry; for this my son was dead, and is alive again; he was lost and is found.' And they began to be merry" (Luke 15:20, 22-24).

Part Four

THE PARABLE OF THE LOST BROTHER

Now his elder brother was in the field; and as he came and drew near to the house, he heard music and dancing. And he called one of the servants and asked what this meant. And he said to him, "Your brother has come, and your father has killed the fatted calf, because he has received him safe and sound." But he was angry and refused to go in. His father came out and entreated him, but he answered his father, "Lo, these many years I have served you, and I never disobeyed your command, yet you never gave me a kid, that I might make merry with my friends. But when this son of yours came, who has devoured your living with harlots, you killed for him the fatted calf!" And he said to him, "Son, you are always with me, and all that is mine is yours. It was fitting to make merry and be glad, for this your brother was dead, and he is alive; he was lost and is found."

Luke 15:25-32

Chapter Thirteen

ЈHE ELDER SON

We usually think of Luke 15 containing three stories—the story of the lost coin, the story of the lost sheep, and the story of the lost boy. In reality, however, there are four stories and the fourth is the parable of the lost brother. Too often and for too long he has been merely a foil for his errant, but more attractive, relative. He has been introduced as part of the dark background that throws the foreground into sharp relief.

Actually, he is far more than that. He is "the prodigal of all prodigals"[136] and, as such, he deserves to be considered in his own right. Certainly to Jesus he was a real person and, what is more important, there is something of his spirit in us all. Thus in an assembly of ministers at Elberfeldt the question was asked, "Who is the prodigal's brother?" To which Daniel Krummacher replied, "I know him very well: I met him yesterday." "Who is he?" they inquired. To which he answered, "Myself!"[137]

It should be noted that he was the elder son. He was the prodigal's older brother and as such enjoyed a position of privilege. The right of succession was legally his so it was assumed that he would eventually become the head of the family just as the Prince of Wales will ascend to the throne of

England upon the abdication or death of his mother, Queen Elizabeth. That was the prize which Jacob coveted and which Esau sold him for a mess of pottage (Genesis 25:29-34). Moreover, as the eldest son, he was entitled to a double portion of the family inheritance, which, in this case, would be two thirds of his father's estate (Deuteronomy 1:17). Whatever the prodigal received, he would receive twice as much. So when the father said, "All that is mine is yours" (Luke 15:31), he was telling the truth because the prodigal had already received his portion.

Yet, even more important than that, was the pledge that God's blessing would rest upon him as the first-born. It was because Esau scorned that blessing that the writer of Hebrews describes him as "immoral or irreligious" (Hebrews 12:16), for it marked him as a man of the world, as one who enjoyed both the comforts of life and material things but who gave little thought to the promises of God. In contrast, those who are spiritually minded, those who realize that "here we have no abiding city but we seek one to come" (Hebrews 13:14), those who know that "the Most High rules the kingdom of men" (Daniel 4:17) and that we are surrounded by a spiritual world from which we draw strength and hope,[138] consider those "blessings" to be the most significant part of the elder son's inheritance.

Biologically speaking, most of us are not "elder sons"; we are not the first-born of our families but, like the prodigal's brother, we have been highly favored. We have been granted "elder son" status. We have been blessed with health and strength. We live in a land of peace and prosperity. We have certain inalienable rights—freedom of speech, freedom of assembly, and freedom to worship. We have significant opportunities for growth and development and, above all, we have the word of the Gospel, the means of grace and the hope of glory!

So, like him, we should be dutiful sons. The prodigal's brother claimed as much. "Lo, these many years I have served you" (Luke 15:29) and his claim is supported by the facts. He was a hard worker. He did not loll about the house as "the heir presumptive" but laboured in the fields along with the hired servants. He worked long hours, coming home only in the evening when darkness had settled over the land. It is quite unlikely that the father threw a party in the daytime; yet when the elder son drew near to the house, the music and dancing were already in progress. That should make it clear that he was not a man to watch "the clock" but one who laboured hard from dawn 'til dusk! He was a hard worker and he was an exemplary young man. He stayed close to home. His friends were eminently respectable. There is no evidence of loose living in his record. He did not "waste his substance in riotous living" (Luke 15:13 KJV). Far from "sowing his wild oats" he was a paragon of virtue. And, with it all, he was obedient. Like the rich young ruler he could say of his father's commands, "All these I have observed from my youth" (Mark 12:20). He was a dutiful son, a most commendable young man!

There are many today who could make the same claim. They can say with sincerity and without undue arrogance that they have tried to live respectable lives, that they have striven to keep the laws of God, and that they have endeavoured to be both good parents and upstanding citizens. But, dutiful sons may not be true sons. Such was the case here. The prodigal's brother "bore the name of a son, but he carried the heart of a servant."[139] He was known by the family name but his heart did not beat in harmony with his father's heart.

He lacked a sense of gratitude.   There was no recognition of his privileged position, no acknowledgment of his blessings, no suggestion of thanksgiving for all that he had received. He took those things as a matter of course; he received them as his due, as his personal right. He lacked a sense of gratitude and he had a mercenary spirit.   His relationship to his father was servile rather than filial. He worked not out of a desire to please his father but in order to gain a reward. He laboured not because he was a son but in order to be a son! And, through it all, he toiled under a galling sense of injustice that somehow he had not been treated properly. "You never gave me a kid that I might make merry with my friends" (Luke 15:29).

He lacked a sense of gratitude, he had a mercenary spirit, and he was a surly soul. In *Robert Falconer,* George Macdonald makes the hero read the whole parable to the dying souter. Hearing it, he cried, "O Lord, I'm comin' hame as fast 's I can; but my sins are just like muckle bauchles [shoes down at the heel] upon my feet, and winna lat me. I expec' nae ring and nae robe but I wad fain hae a fiddle I' my grup when the neist prodigal comes hame!"[140] There was nothing of that "sweet, sweet spirit" of forgiveness and joy in the heart of the elder son. There was no appreciation of his father's joy that the lost was found; there was only scathing condemnation and self-righteous pride! "But when this son of yours came, who has devoured your living with harlots, you killed for him the fatted calf !" (Luke 15:30).

The elder brother was no true son.[141] That much is

apparent to us all but can we claim to be any better? Are our hearts full of gratitude and thanksgiving to God for all His goodness to us? Are we one with the Psalmist when he says, "Oh that men would praise the Lord for His goodness, and for His wonderful works to the children of men!" (Psalm 107:8 KJV). Do we serve God out of a sense of duty and obligation or because we want to please Him and rejoice to do His will? Are we one with the Father in His joyful spirit of pardon and redemption? Too often the answer is no! Ours is the spirit of the elder son!

> God's thoughts are not as ours—we gird our breast
> With the cold iron of complacent pride;
> Our charities and kindness are comprest
> With earth's hard bands, that check our loves soft tide;
> And we to sinners say, with scornful brow,
> 'Stand off, for I am holier than thou.'[142]

The prodigal's brother was no true son but he could have been a real son. That is the point of the parable. Certainly the father was as eager for the elder son's return as he was for the prodigal to come home. When the elder son "was angry and refused to go in" (Luke 15:28), "his father came out and entreated him" (Luke 15:28), begged him to join in the festivities. There was no hindrance, no barrier, no prevention on the father's side. The young man could have gone in to the feast. He could have enjoyed the fellowship and he could have been one with his father and his brother in redemptive joy! He could have been a real son!

That is true of us all. God is a God of great compassion and of tender mercy. In sending His Son to be our Savior He has met every requirement of the law, torn down every barrier that hinders, so that now, "whosoever will may come."

> 'Whosoever will! Whosoever will!'
> Send the proclamation over vale and hill;
> 'Tis a loving Father calls the wand'rer home:
> 'Whosoever will may come!'[143]

That suggests the story of Andrew Duncannon. He accepted Christ and joined the church late in life, and he nursed the bitter regret that he did not come sooner. When he was but a lad he heard Dwight L. Moody preach in London. "I shall never forget that night," he said. "Mr. Moody preached on "Seek ye first the kingdom of God and His righteousness, and all these things shall be added unto you" (Matthew 6:33). It seemed to me that night that the gates of the Kingdom stood wide open before me and that both earth and heaven were urging me to enter. I really meant at that moment to have done so but somehow I allowed the occasion to slip by. I drifted out with the crowd and it was nearly fifty years before I became a Christian. God is very pitiful and of wondrous mercy but life can never be what it might have been if I had done what I meant to have done that night!"[144] That is the point. By God's grace we can all be true sons, but only if we "arise and go to our Father!" (Luke 15:18).

Chapter Fourteen

THE ANGRY BROTHER

There is more to be said about the prodigal's brother than was said in the last chapter, for he is portrayed not only as the elder son but also as the angry brother. That he was angry we know but what was he angry about?

We can all understand why the prodigal was angry with himself. He had played the fool. He had sowed the wind and he was reaping the whirlwind (Hosea 8:7). He had brought loss and injury to himself. He had ruined his health in riotous living. He had squandered his inheritance so that now he had nothing. And he had lost not only his reputation but, what was far more damaging, his own sense of self respect.

More than that, he had harmed his friends, those with whom he consorted in the far country. He had helped to pull them down. He had given them a push along the road to destruction. He had cast a shadow of evil upon them. Indeed, how often in moments of reflection and remembrance, he must have thought of his erstwhile companions and wondered about their fate and where they were.

He had reason to be angry with himself. He had injured himself, he had harmed others and he had brought sorrow to his father's heart. There was the hurt caused by his departure. There was the anguish of his long absence and there was the grief occasioned by his return—the tears shed not in public but in private—because of his sorry appearance and his poor condition.

We can all understand that but why was the elder brother so angry and upset? What harm or injury did the prodigal do to him? It was the prodigal's health that was undermined, not his. It was the prodigal's friends that were injured, not those whom he claimed as his own. Why then was the elder brother so difficult and unreasonable?

The answer to that, strange as it may sound, is jealousy. The elder brother was jealous of the prodigal. Does that sound preposterous? In some ways it does. After all, the elder brother still had his inheritance intact while the prodigal had wasted his in riotous living. The elder brother enjoyed a good reputation while the prodigal son was regarded as a wastrel. And the elder brother was surrounded by his friends while the prodigal's friends were long since gone and far away. In sum, the elder brother had so much and the prodigal now had so little. Why then was the elder brother jealous? What was there to be jealous about?

This, to begin with. The elder son was jealous of his brother's courage. After all it takes a certain amount of independence and initiative to defy tradition and to go one's way regardless of the consequences.[145] Those qualities—a willingness to step out of line and a readiness to stand alone—the prodigal possessed and the elder brother was jealous because they were missing in his life. Secretly he had often wanted to "kick over the traces," and sow his wild oats, and plow his own furrow but he lacked the strength to do it.

So he envied his brother's courage and he was jealous of his brother's fun. He knew, what many of us deny, that there is fun in the far country. If such was not the case prodigals would not go there time after time. There is excitement and exhilaration in the bright lights, and the brazen women, and the brassy music. There in the far country there is the thrill of adventure and the tang of danger. There is something there that titillates the senses and inflames the imagination and excites the mind. There is novelty and camaraderie and fellowship. To be sure the next day reaction may set in—there may be regret, and remorse and resentment—but there is no denying that, at the time, there is fun in the far country and the elder brother was jealous, envious of that fun.

After all, his own life had been pretty drab and humdrum. He had stayed at home and done the chores and, preoccupied with work and loaded down with responsibility, he had neglected the social graces which could have added zest and color to his life. In fact, if the truth be told, he seems to have denied himself the legitimate pleasures and satisfactions which life offers us all. So far as we know he never married, never had a family or even spent time enjoying the companionship of others. He was a loner who secretly wanted to be loved. He was a drudge who longed for the delights which life contains. So, oppressed by the dulness of his own existence, he lashed out at his brother. He showed resentment because he was jealous of his brother's courage and of the good times which his brother had enjoyed.

Yes, and he was jealous of the love which his father had for the younger boy. There is no doubt that the father loved the prodigal, loved him in spite of everything. After all he was his son, and he was attractive—personality wise, far more attractive than his hard working, respectable brother. Moreover, knowing the danger that lurked in the far country, the father was concerned for the younger boy's welfare and safety. So he yearned for him, and prayed for him, and watched day after dreary day for his return.

The father certainly loved his prodigal son but that does not mean that he did not love the elder brother. He did but somehow the older boy kept him at bay. He built a wall of reserve around himself. He went about his duties, he gave his father proper respect but their communications were strained and formal. There was little real fellowship and communion between them. Yet, paradoxically, the elder son wanted his father's love and, failing to secure it, he resented the love which his father had for the prodigal.

In all that, the one thing the elder brother needed to realize, as do all of us, is that there is no need for jealousy. The elder son had no reason to be jealous of his younger brother. After all, if it takes courage to go wrong it takes more courage to do what is right. The elder son saw the courage of his brother in stepping out of line, and scattering his reputation, and burning his bridges behind him, and he felt, quite properly, that he could not do that.

That, however, was no reason to be jealous of his brother's courage or for him to conclude that he was a coward, for there is more than one kind of courage and we all have to choose between them. There is the courage born of passion and desire and the prodigal chose that. There is also what we call moral courage and of the two the latter is both nobler and more demanding. Real courage clothes itself with righteousness not with evil. It is not the servant of impulse but of understanding and the elder brother was free to exercise that virtue to the full.

That is something which we all need to realize. If it takes courage to go wrong it takes more courage to do what is right. It takes courage to repel temptation and it takes courage to stand for the right particularly when righteousness is unpopular and we have to stand alone. In the words of the old hymn—

> Dare to be a Daniel!
> Dare to stand alone!
> Dare to have a purpose firm!
> Dare to make it known![146]

It also needs to be said that if the elder brother did not need to be jealous of the prodigal's courage neither did he need to be jealous of his brother's fun, for there is fun, real pleasure and satisfaction in the father's house. The fun of the far country is a fleeting, transitory thing which is soon gone and which often leaves in its wake the dust of regret and the ashes of remorse. That is apparent in the story of the prodigal.

On the other hand the happiness of the Father's "house" is an abiding thing for there is love there, and fellowship, and peace and joy. The happiest people are not those who are out enjoying the sights and sounds of the far country but those who love God and seek to do His will, those who respect their fellows and strive to bless and enrich their lives. Here is the testimony of one such soul:

Now none but Christ can satisfy,
None other name for me,
There's love, and life, and lasting joy,
Lord Jesus, found in Thee.[147]

Still further, there was no need for the elder son to be jealous of his brother for there was room in the father's heart for them both. The parable makes that crystal clear for talking with his elder son the father said, "Son, you are always with me" (Luke 15:31). The word the father used there is not the ordinary Greek word for son but the more intimate word *child*. Perhaps the most appropriate rendering would be *Laddie*. "Laddie, you are always with me" (Luke 15:31).

There was room in the father's heart for both the prodigal and for the elder son. That is the message of the parable and that is the heart of the Gospel. There is a story about a prince who sent his fiancée a little golden case with her monogram engraved on it. One day while showing it to a friend she accidently touched a hidden spring and the case flew open to reveal at its heart a priceless jem.[148] This parable of the loving father is such a golden casket and the good news of God's grace for all His children is the jewel at its heart. "In this is love, not that we loved God but that He loved us and sent His Son to be the expiation for our sins" (1 John 4:10). That means that He sent His Son for all of us. In other words, there is room in God's heart not only for the Jew but also for the Gentile. There is room not only for the good but also for the bad. There is room for all who will come. "He who comes to me I will not cast out" (John 6:37).

There was no need for the elder brother to be jealous of the prodigal and there is no need for us to be jealous of others either. After all, jealousy is foolish because none of us really knows the other man's situation. We may long to have his wealth, or his position, or his ability but are we fully cognizant of all his problems and are we willing to shoulder all his responsibilities?

Take the case of Joseph in the Old Testament. We might want to be the controller of Egypt, but in order to get there are we willing to suffer what Joseph suffered—betrayal, slavery, imprisonment and neglect? Or look at David, the shepherd king of Israel. He is an attractive figure and his kingdom is imposing We would all like to stand in David's shoes but are we ready to shoulder his trials—to be a fugitive, and an exile and an outcast? Still further, take the prodigal. If you just look at the adventure, and the glamour, and the father's love he is the most appealing of men but who wants to carry his guilt, and his remorse, and who would voluntarily take upon himself the marks of the far country and bear them for the rest of his life?

There is no need to be jealous of others because jealousy is foolish and because jealousy is destructive. Oftentimes it only makes things worse. Thus the Greeks have an old story which reminds us that jealousy can do irreparable harm. It is the account of a beautiful girl named *Procris* who fell in love with a mighty hunter called *Cephalus*. In her jealousy she begrudged him the time he spent in the woods and as her jealousy deepened she questioned his loyalty. One day she followed him into the woods and hid in a tree to watch. Returning from the hunt Cephalus was hot and he called on the breeze to come and cool him. Procris, thinking that he was calling to her imagined rival, turned to see her. At that, Cephalus, noticing the moving branches, let fly with his javelin which killed the girl he loved so dearly and the girl who loved him so deeply.[149]

Jealousy can make things worse and, even if it doesn't, it will not do any good. It is futile, useless, of no avail. The truth of the matter is that if we put the same effort into dealing constructively with our relationships, instead of fostering jealousy, we would fare far better. Michelangelo was famous in his earlier years as a sculptor not as a painter. A rival, actuated by professional jealousy, induced the Pope to commission Michelangelo to paint the ceiling of the Sistine Chapel. Convinced that Michelangelo's skill as a painter was not up to his skill as a sculptor the rival felt sure that it would mean his ruin. Michelangelo accepted the commission, worked at it for four years and produced "the mightiest series of paintings the world has ever seen."[150] In fact, it was the Sistine Chapel which established Michelangelo's fame as a painter for all time. It could be the same with us. Instead of indulging in jealousy which is futile we would do better to put our effort into improving our lot and changing our situation.

That is easy to say but what do you do when the "green-eyed monster" comes stealing into your heart? How do you overcome jealousy? By realizing that jealousy is a spiritual problem. It is a lack of faith in God's wisdom and love; a failure to trust His ordering of our lives. What then is the cure? It is prayer. "Create in me a clean heart, O God, and renew a right spirit within me!" (Psalm 51:10). Then, renewed in spirit, we need to "make merry and be glad" (Luke 15:32).

Chapter Fifteen

THE FATHER'S HOUSE

The father's house must have been a wonderful place. After all, it was the expression of the father's love, the evidence of the father's wealth, and the embodiment of the father's spirit. There was comfort there for we are told that there were servants and that suggests some degree of affluence. There was affection there for when the prodigal returned and asked that he might be taken on as "a hired servant" (Luke 15:19)—the lowest rank of all[151]—he was given the best robe, a ring was put on his finger and shoes on his feet. Above all, there was joy there. The atmosphere was one of happiness and harmony. Indeed, when the elder son drew near to the house he heard music and dancing. In the original both words are interesting for the word for *music* is our word *symphony* and suggests a band of musicians[152] while the word for *dancing* is our word *chorus* and may imply the presence of a troop or band.[153] The atmosphere of the father's house was one of love and abundance and rejoicing.

Can we not say the same about the "house" which our Heavenly Father has given us here? One thinks of the world of nature in which He has placed us. There, on every side, we see evidence of His wisdom and tokens of His love. We see it in the preparation which He made for our coming. "When life appears," writes Macniele Dixon in his stimulating book *The Human Situation,* "it appears in a world that somehow supports it."[154] Life in all its forms depends upon nutrition and nutrition is available. Life can exist only within narrow limits of temperature and those limits have been maintained through millions of years. Moreover, life could not continue if the impulse to mate were lacking, and though biology offers no explanation, it is there. God has prepared for our coming and, beyond that preparation, His love is evident in the added touches of majesty and beauty which constantly surround us. We see it in the golden beauty of the sunset, in the cerulean blue of the sky, in the trees and mountains clothed in their coats of many colors, in the star-studded vault of the heavens, and in the peaceful flow of some gentle stream. Truly—

> This is my Father's world,
> And to my listening ears
> All nature sings, and round me rings,
> The music of the spheres.
> This is my Father's world;
> I rest me in the thought
> Of rocks, and trees, of skies, and seas
> His hand the wonders wrought.[155]

The outside of our Father's "house" is splendid to our view but there is more inside. There is a house in Bruges which has a motto on a rafter near the front door. It reads, "There is more inside."[156] So it is here. When we go inside that house and experience the wonder of human love, and the joy of family life, and the blessings of society, we become even more conscious of the richness of the Father's "house."

Nor is that all. What shall we say about the fellowship

of the Church, "the fellowship of kindred minds which is like to that above"?[157] In his little book, *Iron Shoes,* Roy Angell tells of a visit he received one evening from the pastor of a nearby church. Angell invited him in, asking him what he was doing out on such a cold winter night. The man replied that he had just seen something that he wanted to share with his brother minister before he went home.

Then he told Roy Angell how his church cared for an elderly widow who lived at the foot of the hill. Fearing that she might need some assistance on that particular night the pastor said that he had gone to see her. Upon entering the house he saw a basket of groceries on the table and a man's greatcoat lying across a chair. "Where is he, Auntie?" he asked banteringly. "You've got a man hidden around here somewhere. Trot him out!" Cheerily she led the minister to the kitchen window and, looking out, he saw the President of the seminary chopping wood over by the woodshed.[158] The fellowship of the church! What a wonderful thing it is when it is not artificial or contrived but spontaneous and genuine.

> We share each other's woes,
> Each other's burdens bear;
> And often for each other flows
> The sympathizing tear.[159]

But enough of this "house" in which you and I are privileged to live. Come back to the home in our parable and note that into the harmony and happiness of that father's house the elder son introduced a discordant note. "And he [the elder son] called one of the servants and asked what this [this festivity] meant. And he said to him, 'Your brother has come, and your father has killed the fatted calf, because he has received him safe and sound.' But he was angry and refused to go in" (Luke 15:26-28a).

He was uncharitable, quite unwilling to forgive and to forget what his brother had done. On one occasion Abraham Lincoln was asked how he was going to treat the rebellious southerners when they were defeated and had returned to the Union. His answer is classic. "I will treat them as if they had never been away."[160] There is nothing of that spirit in the elder son. He was uncharitable, unforgiving! "He was angry and would not go in" (Luke 15:28a KJV).

He was uncharitable and he was ungrateful, unappreciative of what his father had done for him. To be sure, he had served his father faithfully, but the work was done grudgingly and of necessity, not in a spirit of love and thankfulness. When Robert Louis Stevenson lived in the South Sea Islands he had a native boy who always woke him in the morning for tea and toast. One day that particular boy was ill and another lad took his place. He woke Stevenson not only for tea and toast but also for a beautifully cooked omelette. When Stevenson saw it, he said to the lad, "Boy, great is your wisdom." "No, Master," replied the servant, "but great is my love!"[161] That sense of indebtedness and appreciation was foreign to the elder son. All he could say was, "Lo, these many years I have served you, and I never disobeyed your command; yet you never gave me a kid that I might make merry with my friends!" (Luke 15:29).

He was uncharitable, and ungrateful, and uncomprehending. He was totally insensitive to his brother's plight, indifferent both to what he had gone through and to what he had lost. He shows no understanding of what his brother must have suffered, suffered both physically and psychologically, there in the far country. There is no indication that he realized, not only the hunger which his brother must have endured but, what was far worse, the bitter remorse and poignant shame which must have engulfed him. Nor is there anything to suggest that he appreciated the price which his brother had paid for his folly and would continue to pay in the years to come. The prodigal's legal position was clear. He was his father's son, but he had nothing and he could expect nothing in the future.

In that ancient world there were two ways in which property might pass from father to son—by a will or by a gift during the father's life. In the latter case the general rule was that the beneficiary received possession of the land but could not sell it, and the fruit of the land belonged to the father until he died.[162]   In the case of the younger son that rule was apparently waived. He demanded and was given not only the right of possession but also the right of disposal. He received the price of the land and he disposed of it. "He wasted his substance with riotous living" (Luke 15:13 KJV). "He spent everything" (Luke 15:14). As a result he had nothing left and nothing to look forward to. Everything belonged to his brother. The elder son must have known that but he seems to have been quite unmoved and untroubled by his brother's plight.

We have all been quick to condemn the elder son, and rightly so, but there is something of his spirit in us all. Like him we have spoiled the atmosphere and disturbed the harmony of our Father's "house." We have polluted the world of nature. We have upset its delicate balance through our greed and through our indifference to the rights of others. We have ruined our lakes and rivers by making them the repositories of our waste materials and we have scarred our hills and mountains with our surface mining and our lack of reforestation. As a result our world is no longer a "Garden of Eden." It reflects and mirrors our estrangement both from God and from one another.

But that is not all. If we have polluted the world of nature we have also perverted the blessings of society. We have used God's good gifts not for the enrichment of our own lives and for the good of others but for personal gratification and for selfish ends. As a consequence there is fear and tension and misunderstanding and estrangement in our relationships, the one with the other. It is Ernest Campbell who tells the story of two men who lived in a houseboat tied to a waterfront dock. One night, while they slept, a storm came up. The boat broke its moorings and drifted out to sea. Next morning one of the men got up early and went out on deck. He was both surprised and shocked. Rushing to rouse his friend he cried, "Wake up, wake up, we're not here anymore."[163] How true that is! We are not where we should be and we are not where God meant us to be! We are not —

One great fellowship of love,
Throughout the whole wide earth.[164]

We are but an armed camp which views others with suspicion and dread.

Like the elder son we have disturbed the harmony of our Father's "house." We have polluted the world of nature, we have perverted the blessings of society and we have poisoned the fellowship of the church with our selfishness and lack of love. Carlyle Marney hints at that in one of his famous stories. "Everywhere I go," he said, "people ask me why I remain a Baptist. Being a Baptist is like being in a dark, slimy well: it's cold, clammy, uncomfortable and filled with lots of creepy things. For years I have tried to climb out but it was hard. The walls were slippery. I was half blind and there were impediments everywhere. Finally, however, I reached the top. I looked around to see what the world was like in the other denominations. And when I had a good look—I just dropped back into the well."[165] Surely one needs to say no more.

In spite of that, our Father's "house" can be, by God's grace, "a thing of beauty and a joy forever."[166] Where there is hatred there can be love. Where there is tension there can be peace. Where there is aimlessness there can be purpose. Where there is sin there can be pardon. Where there is bondage there can be freedom. Where there is unhappiness there can be joy. And where there is despair there can be hope.

It all depends on one thing—whether the spirit that is in us is the spirit of the elder brother or the spirit of the loving father. In the parable the father came out and entreated the elder son to come in but he refused. "He was angry and refused to go in."

Chapter Sixteen

A FITTING CELEBRATION

"It was fitting to make merry and be glad for this, your brother, was dead and is alive; he was lost and is found" (Luke 15:32). That is not a statement open to further discussion but a judgment which concludes the matter. In spite of that, the elder son saw nothing fitting in this celebration. The prodigal did not deserve it for he had come home in disgrace and the community did not want it for to them it appeared scandalous—a reward for sin and an encouragement to prodigal living.

As the elder son saw it there was nothing fitting about this celebration and, from where he stood, he was right. Judged by human standards that celebration was anything but proper and to claim differently is to misunderstand our Lord's words, for in the original the word fitting suggests not so much the idea of propriety as it does the thought of necessity.[167] What Jesus actually said was, "Proper or not, it is necessary that we make merry and be glad for this your brother was dead, and is alive; he was lost and is found" (Luke 15:32). That statement concludes the parable and there are two reasons why we should agree with its evaluation.

The first is that the celebration was necessary for the prodigal's rehabilitation. He had sinned and now, chastened and repentant, had come home seeking not only food for his body but, what was even more important, sustenance for his soul. He had come home looking for love and forgiveness, longing for acceptance. It was not that he deserved it but rather that he needed it, for forgiveness is "the most therapeutic idea in the world,"[168] and it brings with it health and healing!

Ian Maclaren offers us a touching instance of that in *The Days of Auld Lang Syne.* Charlie Grant, to whom we have already made reference, comes home to find that there is no one to receive his repentance, no one to stretch out to him a hand, no one to bid him go in peace. Despondent and discouraged he is about to leave again when Drumsheugh finds him and bids him welcome, tells him about the prayers offered by his mother and grandmother on his behalf, and how they died believing that he would return. Those words of greeting—that welcome, and that encouragement from the past—were the words Charlie Grant needed for, knowing that he was accepted, he went on his way rejoicing.[169] It was the same with the prodigal. He needed that celebration as a token of his father's forgiveness and as an expression of his family's love.

But that celebration was necessary not only for the prodigal's restoration but also for the father's well being. His joy at his boy's return had to find expression and his love for his son had to be vented. It was a necessity of his nature.

Truett Rogers, a preacher from the mountain state of West Virginia, tells of an experience like that in his own life. As a lad he was constantly getting into trouble. One day his mother picked him up after school so that he could deliver packages of printed material to customers. She was not smiling and he assumed the worst. It was something he had done and she had found out about it. He says that, sitting behind the steering wheel, she drove down the street in the direction of the reform school. It was more than he could stand and suddenly he burst into tears. Dismayed, his mother pulled over to the side of the road saying, "What's the matter with you?" Truett's only response was to ask her if she was taking him to the reform school. She replied by taking him in her arms and saying, "Truett, remember this always; don't ever forget it. I know that you are naughty and that you get into a lot of trouble, and we have to discipline you but, if you do the worst thing imaginable, if you have to go to prison, if one day they sentence you to the gallows for hanging, on the way up the steps look around and your mama will be right behind you!"[170]

Love for her son was an essential part of her being, it was a necessity of her nature, and it was the same with the prodigal's father. The celebration was fitting—it was a necessity of his father heart!

That celebration was necessary, both for the prodigal and for the prodigal's father, but what does it add to the message of the parable? It guarantees our welcome. There is an old story about a lad who went wrong and disgraced his family and served time in the penitentiary. Now, released from prison, he is on his way home but, unsure of his welcome, he sent his parents this brief message. "If you want me to come home, tie a white rag on the tree beside the railroad tracks." As the train approached his destination the lad wondered if there would be a rag on the tree. "If there is not a rag," he said to himself, "I'll just keep on going!" Then the conductor called "Smithville" and he saw it. His eyes filled with tears for the tree was full of rags![171] In the same way these festivities witness to the welcome that awaits us when we too turn towards home.

These festivities tell us that even now our heavenly Father waits to welcome us. Colin Wilson once declared that "the answers of religion are the lies we tell to make ourselves comfortable."[172] Frankness like that is commendable but the statement is wrong, all wrong. The evidence of God's unchanging and unceasing love for us is both clear and convincing. We see it in the history of the Jews, in God's willingness to pardon their iniquities and to bring them back from the land of Babylon. "Comfort, comfort my people," says your God. "Speak tenderly to Jerusalem and cry to her that her warfare is ended, that her iniquity is pardoned, that she has received from the Lord's hand double for all her sins" (Isaiah 40:1-2).

We see God's love in the history of the Jews and we see it in the death of Jesus Christ for us sinners. "God shows His love for us in that while we were yet sinners Christ died for us" (Romans 5:8). To say that is to say that Christ died in our place and in our stead and to speak in that way implies substitution,[173] such as is recorded in the story of Schamyl, the chief of the fierce heroes of the Caucasus in their long struggle against the Russians. At one time, so the story goes, some unknown traitor was giving away the secrets of Schamyl's little band, and he gave an order that the next person found communicating with the enemy in any way should be scourged. Eventually the culprit was discovered and it was Schamyl's mother. For two days Schamyl disappeared within his tent. Then he emerged, worn out with his misery and shame. He bade his men strip him and bind him to the stake and bind him to the stake and scourge him, instead of his mother, with the knout.[174] It is true that analogies from human experience do not resolve the mystery of the crucifixion. They serve only to state it but, if Christ's death is in any way substitutionary, it is the supreme expression of God's love for us.

Nor is that all. We see that love for us in the history of the Jews, in the death of Christ for us, and in the life of the Church, for there, in century after century and in generation after generation, we see men convicted by the Holy Spirit, convinced of God's pardon and sent on their way rejoicing.

Thus Lesslie Newbigin speaks for multitudes when he writes, "I still see the cross of Jesus as the one place in the history of human culture where there is a final dealing with the ultimate mysteries of sin and forgiveness, of bondage and freedom, of conflict and peace, of death and life. Although there is so much that is puzzling, so much that I simply do not understand and so much that is unpredictable, I find here—as I have again and again found during the past fifty years—a point from which one can take one's bearings and a light in which one can walk, however, stumblingly."[175]

Our heavenly Father loves us and even now He waits to welcome us no matter who we are or what we have done. That is our Christian Faith. That is the Good News which the New Testament proclaims and that is why Christianity is the most joyous of religions. Yes, and that is why we sing—

Come, ye sinners, poor and wretched,
Weak and wounded, sick and sore;
Jesus ready stands to save you,

Full of pity joined with power:
He is able, He is able,
He is willing; doubt no more.

Come, ye needy, come and welcome,
God's free bounty glorify;
True belief and true repentance,
Every grace that brings you nigh,
Without money, without money,
Come to Jesus Christ and buy.

Lo! the incarnate God, ascended,
Pleads the merit of His blood;
Venture on Him, venture wholly,
Let no other trust intrude:
None but Jesus, none but Jesus,
Can do helpless sinners good![176]

What do these festivities, celebrating the prodigal's return, add to the message of the parable? They tell us that even now the heavenly Father waits to welcome us and they assure us a welcome in the Father's house. Some of you may wonder about that, and you have good reason for doing so, because the spirit of the elder brother has sometimes prevailed in the life of the Church. Thus Jesus found that spirit of self-righteous pride, which condemns some and excludes others, in the Jewish Church, for that was the spirit of the Scribes and Pharisees who opposed him.And that spirit is by no means dead today. God's willingness to forgive and to cast our sins into the depths of the sea (Micah 7:19) is a light which shines forth into the darkness of our "naughty world."[177] There are those in our day, however, who have taken that light from the window of the Church and refuse to put it back. In spite of that, and regardless of the positions which they hold and the influence which they yield, you need to know that they are no true members of the Father's house, for where the Spirit of Christ abides the prodigal always receives a welcome when he returns.

Paul discovered that when, following his conversion, he came to the church in Jerusalem, for Barnabas "took him, and brought him to the apostles, and declared to them how on the road he had seen the Lord, who spoke to him, and how at Damascus he had preached boldly in the name of Jesus. So he went in and out among them at Jerusalem, preaching boldly in the name of the Lord" (Acts 9:27-29).

Prodigals are always welcome in the Christian Church. Paul discovered that and so did Augustine. After a sojourn in the Far Country he was converted in the city of Milan after which the Church not only received him but called him to preach the word of God.[178]

Paul and Augustine discovered that prodigals are welcome in the Father's house, and so will prodigals today when they come to themselves and set out for home. John Everland discovered that when he came to the First Baptist Church in St. Paul, Minnesota, asking for money so that he could pick up a shirt at the local Chinese laundry. The story proved to be a hoax but, under the guidance of the Pastor, Dr. Edwin T. Dahlberg, he made a confession of faith in Jesus Christ as Savior and Lord. Later, he was baptized and joined the Church and, as part of that fellowship, became not only an outstanding Christian but also a Deacon and a Sunday School teacher.[179]

There will always be a few who will resent the presence of prodigals in the Church, but the real problem today is not that the Church refuses to receive prodigals but that prodigals so often are unwilling to come to the Church. They assume that they are not wanted and that they will be turned away, but if they will only come they will be welcomed and will discover for themselves the warmth of Christian love. They will find that all along the door has been open, open for them to come. That is the point of the old Hasidic tale of the Jew who year after year sat before the gate of the king, waiting to be admitted for an audience. At last, grown old with age, he asked the guard, "When may I go in?" To which the guard replied, "For you, this gate has always been open!" That applies to prodigals. For them the door is always open!

The festivities which marked the prodigal's return tell us that our heavenly Father waits to welcome us, they assure us of a welcome in the Father's house and they anticipate the welcome that awaits us in the Father's house above. That such a welcome does await us there should be no doubt. The Scriptures proclaim it. "Goodness and mercy shall follow me all the days of my life; and I shall dwell in the house of the Lord for ever" (Psalm 23:6). Our Lord confirms it. "In my Father's house are many rooms; if it were not so would I have told you that I go to prepare a place for you? And when I go and prepare a place for you, I will come again and will take you to myself, that where I am there you may be also" (John 14:1-3). And the resurrection anticipates it. "Christ has been raised from the dead, the first fruits of those who have fallen asleep" (1 Corinthians 15:20).

It is the assurance of that welcome which shines

through the story of John Todd. He was born in Rutland, Vermont, in October 1800. Shortly afterward his family moved to Connecticut and settled in the little community of Killingworth. There, when John was only six years old, both his parents died. The children had to be parceled out among the kind-hearted relatives and John was assigned to an aunt who lived ten miles away in the village of North Killingworth. He lived with her until he went away to study at Yale College and later prepare for the ministry. When he was in his early forties and minister of the Congregational Church in Pittsfield, Massachusetts, his aunt—now a woman of advanced years—fell seriously ill. In great distress of mind she wrote to her beloved nephew. Suppose she died: what would death be like? Would it mean agony, terror, maybe annihilation? Here is the letter John Todd sent in reply.

"It is now nearly thirty-five years since I, a little boy of six, was left quite alone in the world. You sent me word that you would give me a home, be a kind mother to me. I have never forgotten the day when I made the long journey of ten miles to your home in North Killingworth. I can still recall my disappointment when, instead of coming yourself, you sent your... [servant] Caesar to fetch me. I can still remember my tears and my anxiety as, perched on your horse and clinging tight to Caesar, I started for my new home. Night fell before we finished our journey, and as the darkness deepened I became more and more afraid. Finally I said anxiously to Caesar, 'Do you think she'll go to bed before we get there?' 'O no!' he answered reassuringly. 'She'll sho' stay up fo' you. When we get out of these here woods you'll see her candle, shinin' in her window.' Presently we did ride into a clearing, and there—sure enough—was your candle. I remember that you were waiting at the door of your house, that you put your arms around me, that you lifted me a tired and frightened little boy—down from the horse. There was a fire on your hearth, a warm supper on your stove. Then after supper you took me up to my room, heard me say my prayers, and then sat beside me till I dropped off to sleep.

"You undoubtedly realize why I am now recalling all these things to your mind. Some day soon God may send for you, to take you to a new home. Don't fear the summons, the strange journey, the dark messenger of death. At the end of the road you will find love and a welcome, you will be safe—there as here—in God's love and care. Surely He can be trusted to be as kind to you as you were years ago to me!"[180]

It is a bonny prospect and it is for everyone, for all who leave the far country and come home.

> Come to the Savior now,
> He gently calleth thee;
> In true repentance bow,
> Before Him bend the knee.
> He waiteth to bestow
> Salvation, peace, and love,
> True joy on earth below,
> A home in heaven above.[181]

NOTES

(Notes pages 3-8)

1. George Adam Smith, *The Historical Geography of the Holy Land* (London: Hodder & Stoughton, 1904), pp. 311-12.

2. Joachim Jeremias, "Poimen," *Theological Dictionary of the New Testament,* vol. 6, eds., Gerhard Kittel and Gerhard Friedrich (Grand Rapids: Eerdmans Pub. Co., 1971), p. 490 [Genesis 46:34].

3. Arthur John Gossip, *The Galilean Accent* (Edinburgh: T & T Clark, 1926), pp. 115-16.

4. John D. Freeman, *Life on the Uplands* (Toronto: William Briggs, 1906), p. 73.

5. William Barclay, *The Gospel of Luke* (Philadelphia: The Westminster Press, 1956), p. 206.

6. Martha Stockton, "God Loved the World of Sinners Lost," *The Hymnary* (Toronto: The Ryerson Press, 1936), no. 479.

7. Claude Montefiore, *Synoptic Gospels,* vol. 2 (London: Macmillan & Co., Ltd.), pp. 520-21.

8. Morris West, *The Shoes of the Fisherman* (Nashville: Parthenon Press, 1952), p. 129.

9. Erdmann Neumeister, "Sinners Jesus Will Receive," *The Hymnary* (Toronto: The Ryerson Press, 1936), no. 477.

10. James Hastings, ed., *Great Texts of the Bible* (Edinburgh: T & T Clark, 1912), p. 454.

11.   Bernhard Anderson, *Understanding the Old Testament* (Englewood Cliffs, N.J.: Prentice Hall, 1957), p. 417.

12.   James M. Barrie, *The Little Minister* (New York: Hurst & Co., 1891), p. 338.

13.   Frederick William Faber, "Souls of Men Why Will Ye Scatter?" *The Hymnary* (Toronto: The Ryerson Press, 1936), no. 468.

14.   Richard Chenevix Trench, *Notes on the Parables of Our Lord* (New York: Fleming Revell Co.), p. 289. "The wilderness here is no sandy or rocky desert, the haunt of wild beasts or of wandering robber hordes, rather wide, extended grassy plains, steppes of savannahs, called 'desert' because without habitation of men, but exactly the fittest place for the pasture of sheep."

15.   Samuel John Stone, "The Church's One Foundation," *The Hymnary* (Toronto: The Ryerson Press, 1936), no. 164.

16.   Emil Brunner, *Eternal Hope* (Philadelphia: The Westminster Press, 1934), p. 7.

17.   Albert Schweitzer, *Memoirs of Childhood and Youth* (New York: The Macmillan Co., 1963), p. 10.

18.   Richard Chenevix Trench, "Prayer," quoted in *Masterpieces of Religious Verse,* ed., James Dalton Morrison (New York: Fleming Revell & Bros., 1948), no. 1341.

19.   William Barclay, *And Jesus Said* (Philadelphia: The Westminster Press, 1970), p. 179.

20.   The word *pastor* is a translation of the Greek word *poimen* which means a shepherd. The English word *pastor* is a transliteration of the Latin noun *pastor* which comes from the verb *pascere* and means to feed, to lead to pasture, to keep or to nourish.

21.   Oscar Hammerstein, "Ol' Man River" (New York: T. B. Harms, 1927).

22.   Paul Scherer, "The Book of Job," *The Interpreter's Bible,* vol. 3 (Nashville: Abingdon Press, 1954), p. 957.

23.   William Barclay, *Ephesians* (Philadelphia: The Westminster Press, 1958), p. 135.

24.   Elizabeth C. Clephane, "The Ninety and Nine," *Sacred Songs & Solos,* ed., Ira D. Sankey (London: Marshall, Morgan & Scott), no. 97.

25.   Clephane, "Ninety and Nine," stanza 3.

26.   George A. Buttrick, *The Parables of Jesus* (New York: Harper & Bros., 1928), p. 179.

27.   Henry Drummond, *The Ideal Life* (London: Hodder & Stoughton, 1899), p. 48.

28.   Thomas Carlyle, quoted by F. W. Boreham, *Wisps of Wildfire* (New York: Abingdon Press, 1924), p. 197.

29.   Whitney J. Oates, ed. *Basic Writings of St. Augustine,* vol. 1 (New York: Random House, 1948), p. xvii.   See also Roy W. Battenhouse, *A Companion to the Study of St. Augustine* (NewYork: Oxford University Press, 1955), pp. 31-34.

30.   Charles W. Colson, *Born Again* (Old Tappan: Fleming H. Revell, 1976). See also Charles W. Colson, *Life Sentence* (Waco: Word Books, 1979).

31.   William Shakespeare, *Macbeth,* act 5, sc. 1, lines 55-56.

32.   Clephane, "Ninety and Nine, stanza 1.

33.   John Sutherland Bonnell, *What Are You Living For?* (Knoxville: Abingdon-Cokesbury Press, 1940), pp. 24-25.

34.   Joachim Jeremias, *The Parables of Jesus* (New York: Charles Scribner's Sons, 1955), p. 107.

35.   Clephane, "Ninety and Nine," stanza 5.

36.   *The Evangelical Christian* (Toronto: Evangelical Publishers, August 1936), p. 308.

37.   Ibid.

38.   Bernard of Cluny, "Brief Life Is Here Our Portion," pt. 2, stanza 6, *The Hymnary* (Toronto: The Ryerson Press, 1936), no. 463.

39.   A. R. Cousin, "The Sands of Time," stanza 3, *Sacred Songs & Solos,* ed., Ira D. Sankey (London: Marshall, Morgan & Scott), no. 975.

40.   Rufus Jones, *The Radiant Life* (New York: Macmillan Co., 1944), pp. 11-15.

41.   James M. Logan, "Easter Excitement," *Pulpit Digest* (March-April 1973), p. 25.

42.   "Psalm 23:6, The Scottish Paraphrase," stanza 5, *The Hymnary* (Toronto: The Ryerson Press, 1936), no. 637.

43.   Oscar Cullmann, *Peter* (Philadelphia: The Westminster Press, 1953). Cullmann's conclusion is that Peter was the founder of the Church in Rome without being the founder of a visible Church succession.

44.   James S. Flora, "When Two Become One," *Pulpit Digest* (May/June 1973), p. 12.

45.   Whitney J. Oates, *Basic Writings of Saint Augustine,* vol. 1 (New York: Random House Publishers, 1948), p. 3.

46.   Frederick William Faber, "O Come and Mourn With Me Awhile," stanza 4, *The Hymnary* (Toronto: The Ryerson Press, 1936), no. 90.

47.   James Dalton Morrison, ed., *Masterpieces of Religious Verse* (New York: Harper & Row, 1948), no. 184.

48.   Ibid., no. 186.

49.   Ibid.

50.   Paul Tillich, *The Eternal Now* (New York: Charles Scribner's Sons, 1963), p. 111.

51.   George Arthur Buttrick, "The Gospel According to Luke," *The Interpreter's Bible,* vol. 8 (New York: Abingdon Press, 1952), p. 268.

52.   William Barclay, *The Gospel of Luke* (Philadelphia: The Westminster Press, 1956), p. 209.

53.   Joachim Jeremias, *Rediscovering the Parables* (New York: Charles Scribner's Sons, 1966), p. 107.

54.   William Barclay, *Gospel of Luke*, p. 209.

55.   William Barclay, *The Gospel of John,* vol. 2 (Philadelphia: The Westminster Press, 1956), p. 4. Archibald Thomas Robertson, *Word Pictures in the New Testament,* vol. 5 (New York: Harper & Bros., 1932), p. 139. Robertson questions this interpretation and indicates that the use of *katagrapho* "leaves it uncertain whether He was writing words or drawing pictures or making signs."

56.   Albert E. Bailey, *The Gospel in Art* (Boston: Pilgrim Press, 1946), p. 226.

57.   William Barclay, *The Gospel of John,* vol. 2 (Philadelphia: The Westminster Press, 1956), p. 4.

58.   [James Moffatt], *A New Translation of the Bible* (London: Hodder & Stoughton, 1935).

59.   William H. Lecky, *History of European Morals,* vol.1 (New York: D. Appleton & Co., 1869), p. 266.

60.   Rolf Hochhuth, *The Deputy* (New York: Grove Press, 1964), p. 83.

61.   Harry Emerson Fosdick, *On Being a Real Person* (New York: Harper & Bros., 1943), p. 133.

62.   William Shakespeare, *Henry V,* act 3, sc. 2, line 13.

63.   J. Gordon Jones, ed., *Our Baptist Fellowship* (Baptist Convention of Ontario & Quebec, 1939), p. 151.

64.   Roland H. Bainton, *Here I Stand* (New York: Abingdon-Cokesbury Press, 1940), p. 185.

65.   [James Moffatt], *A New Translation of the Bible.*

66.   G. Ernest Wright, "The Book of Deuteronomy," *The Interpreter's Bible,* vol. 2 (New York: Abingdon Press), p. 320, says, "Beginning with Athanasius, Chrysostom, and Jerome in the fourth century A.D., scholars have usually taken this book to be Deuteronomy or some part of it." Gerhard von Rad, *Deuteronomy* (Philadelphia: The Westminster Press, 1966), p. 26, suggests that "one of the sanctuaries of Northern Israel [Shechem or Bethel] was Deuteronomy's place of origin, and the century before 621 B.C. its date."

67.   William Barclay, *The Gospel of John,* vol. 2 (Philadelphia: The Westminster Press, 1956), p. 109.

68.   William Walsham How, "O Word of God Incarnate," stanza 4, *The Hymnary* (Toronto: The Ryerson Press, 1936), no. 182.

69.   William Shakespeare, *Othello,* act 5, sc. 1, line 18.

70.   Charles Nelson Page, *Pictures that Preach* (New York: Abingdon Press n.d.).

71.   John Watson [Ian Maclaren], *Beside the Bonnie Brier Bush* (New York: Dodd & Mead, 1895), p. 151.

72.   George A. Buttrick, *The Parables of Jesus* (New York: Harper & Bros., 1928), p. 182.

73.   Taylor Caldwell, *Great Lion of God* (Greenwich, Connecticut: Fawcett Publications, 1970).

74.   Walter W. Sikes, "The Great New Fact of Our Time," *Revolution and Renewal* (July 1965), p. 4.

75.   Marc Connelly, *The Green Pastures* (New York: Farrar & Rinehart, 1929), p. 69.

76.   Andrew A. Bonar, *Memoirs of McCheyne* (Chicago: Moody Press, 1947), p. 444.

77.   Luke 7: 7-10. Verse 7 uses *pais* (child or servant): verse 10 uses *doulos* (slave).

78.   S. MacLean Gilmour, "The Gospel According to Luke," *The Interpreter's Bible,* vol. 8 (New York: Abingdon Press, n. d.), p. 268.

79.   Joachim Jeremias, *The Parables of Jesus* (New York: Charles Scribner's Sons, 1955), p. 108.

80.   William Barclay, *The Gospel of Luke* (Philadelphia: The Westminster Press, 1956), pp. 209-10.

81.   Joachim Jeremias, *Parables of Jesus,* p. 100.

82.   James S. Stewart, *The Life and Teaching of Jesus Christ* (New York: Abingdon Press), p. 133.

83.   T. Cecil Myers, *Thunder on the Mountain* (Nashville: Abingdon Press, 1965), pp. 96-97.

84.   Behind this phrase, "special possession," there is only one Hebrew word, the word *segullah.* G. A. F. Knight has described beautifully its significance. "In olden days a king was the ultimate owner of everything in the land he ruled. He owned every building, every farm, every coin. Consequently, in his palace, he kept a treasure chest of his 'very own,' in which he delighted to store the precious stones and 'objets d'art' which he loved to handle. This treasure chest was his *segullah.*" [*Law and Grace* (London: S.C.M. Press Ltd., 1962), p. 25.]

85.   Harriet E. Buell, "A Child of the King," *Worship & Service Hymnal* (Chicago: Hope Publishing Co., 1957), no. 309.

86.   Alexander Maclaren, "Luke," in *Expositions of Holy Scripture,* (London: Hodder & Stoughton, 1908), p. 52.

87.   Richard Wright, *Native Son* (New York: Harper & Bros., 1940).

88.   Hendrikus Berkhof, *Christian Faith* (Grand Rapids: William B. Eerdmans Publishing Co., 1979), p. 52.

89.   Ibid., p. 60. "It is not the Spirit who believes in us. We believe, illumined by the Spirit."

90.   Ibid., p. 62.

91.   C. Roy Angell, *Baskets of Silver* (Nashville: The Broadman Press, 1955), pp. 29-30.

92.   Helmut Thielicke, *The Waiting Father* (Cambridge: James Clarke & Co., Ltd., 1978), pp. 17-18.

93.   Harriet E. Buell, "A Child of the King," v.1, *Worship & Service Hymnal* (Chicago: Hope Publishing Co., 1957), no. 309.

94.   James S. Stewart, *The Heralds of God* (Grand Rapids: Baker House, 1979), p. 55.

95.   André Gide, *The Return of the Parable* (London: Sicker & Warburg, 1953), pp. 127-49.

96.   John Watson [Ian Maclaren], *The Days of Auld Lang Syne* (London: Hodder & Stoughton, n.d.), n.p.

97.   Ralph Connor, *The Sky Pilot* (Chicago: Fleming H. Revell Co., 1899), pp. 102-03.

98.   Joachim Jeremias, *The Parables of Jesus* (New York: Charles Scribner's Sons, 1955), p. 104.

99.   James Hastings, ed., *Great Texts of the Bible* (New York: Charles Scribner's Sons, 1913), vol. 10, p. 300.

100.   Joachim Jeremias, *Parables of Jesus*, p. 103.

101.   George A. Buttrick, *The Parables of Jesus* (New York: Harper & Bros., 1928), p. 194.

102.   Kenneth W. Osbeck, *101 Hymn Stories* (Grand Rapids: Pregel Publications, 1992), p. 99.

103.   Samuel Butler, *Hudibras,* pt. 2, canto 1, line 843.

104.   John Watson [Ian Maclaren], *Beside the Bonnie Brier Bush* (New York: Dodd & Mead, 1895), pp. 139-40.

105.   Ibid. , p. 38.

106.   John Fawcett, "Blest Be the Tie that Binds," v.1, *The Hymnary* (Toronto: The Ryerson Press, 1936), no. 376.

107.   Cecil Alexander, "There Is a Green Hill Far Away," v.3, *The Hymnary* (Toronto : The Ryerson Press, 1936), no. 87.

108.   S. MacLean Gilmour, "The Gospel According to Luke," *The Interpreter's Bible,* vol.8 (New York : Abingdon Press), p. 277.

109.   George A. Buttrick, *Parables of Jesus*, p. 194.

110.   George Arthur Buttrick, "The Gospel According to Luke," *The Interpreter's Bible,* vol. 8 (New York: Abingdon Press, 1952), pp . 276-77.

111.   Ibid., p. 277.

112.   Artur Weiser, *The Psalms* (Philadelphia: The Westminster Press, 1962), p. 143.

113.   Anders Nygren, *Agape and Eros* (Philadelphia: The Westminster Press, 1953), pp.75-76. "God's love is altogether spontaneous. It does not look for anything in man that could be adduced as motivation for it."

114. Ibid., pp. 729-30.

115. F. W. Boreham, *The Prodigal* (London: Epworth Press, 1941), pp. 88-89.

116. William J. Thompson, "Softly & Tenderly," *The Hymnary* (Toronto: The Ryerson Press, 1936), no. 494.

117. Charles Dickens, *A Tale of Two Cities* (Boston: Aldine Book Publishing Co.), pp. 116-17.

118. C. Roy Angell, *Baskets of Silver* (Nashville: The Broadman Press, 1955), p. 32.

119. Rudyard Kipling, *The Prodigal Son* (Western Version), stanza 3, line 17.

120. Macniele Dixon, *The Human Situation* (London: Edward Arnold Publishers, 1964), p. 14.

121. Rudyard Kipling, *The Prodigal Son*, stanza 2, lines 9-16, line 43ff.

122. C. Roy Angell, *Baskets of Silver,* p. 31.

123. F. W. H. Myers, *Saint Paul* (Edinburgh: T. N. Foulis Publisher), p. 16.

124. Fyodor Mikhailovitch Dostoievski, *Crime and Punishment* (Bungay: Richard Clay & Co., 1951), p. 542.

125. Ralph Connor, *The Sky Pilot* (Toronto: Fleming H. Revell Co., 1900), pp. 177-79.

126. John Watson [Ian Maclaren], *Beside the Bonnie Brier Bush* (New York: Dodd & Mead, 1895), pp. 151-52.

127. Harry Emerson Fosdick, *On Being a Real Person* (New York: Harper & Bros., 1943), pp. 261-62.

128. Helmut Thielicke, Man in God's World (New York: Harper

& Row, 1963), p. 10.

129.   John Howard Payne, "Home, Sweet Home," from the opera *Clari, the Maid of Milan* (1823).

130.   Halford E. Luccock, *Marching off the Map* (New York: Harper & Bros., 1952), p. 72.

131.   Werner Foerster, *Theological Dictionary of the New Testament,* vol.1 (Grand Rapids: Eerdmans Publishing Co., 1972), p. 507. Foerster points out that *asotia* occurs three times in the New Testament (Ephesians 5:18, Titus 1:6, 1 Peter 4:4) and that in all these passages the word signifies *wild* and *disorderly* rather than extravagant or voluptuous living.

132.   Some records show this is from the writings of George Macdonald.   Uncomfirmed.

133.   Stopford Brooke.   Taken from John S. Whale, *The Protestant Tradition* (Cambridge: The University Press, 1955), p. 22.

134.   William Cowper, "There Is a Fountain," stanza 1.   *The Hymnary* (Toronto: The Ryerson Press, 1936), no. 491.

135.   John Watson [Ian Maclaren], *Beside the Bonnie Brier Bush* (New York: Dodd & Mead, 1895), pp. 157-58.

136.   Paul Scherer, *The Interpreter's Bible n.v.* (New York: Abingdon Press, 1955), p. 911.

137.   James Hamilton, *The Pearl of Parables* (London: Nisbet & Co., 1874), p. 164.

138.   Harry Emerson Fosdick, *A Faith for Tough Times* (New York: Harper & Bros., 1952), p. 98.

139.   Henry Burton, *The Gospel According to St. Luke* (London: Hodder & Stoughton), p. 330.

140.   George Macdonald, *Robert Falconer* (London: Hurst &

Blackett), p. 179.

141   George Arthur Buttrick, "The Gospel According to Luke," *The Interpreter's Bible,* vol. 8 (New York: Abingdon Press, 1952), p. 279, expresses that by saying, "While the prodigal son was prodigal in body, at least part of his heart was always at home; but the elder brother was prodigal at heart, and only his body was at home."

142.   Mrs. T. D. Crewdson, *Poems.* Taken from James Hamilton, *Pearl of Parables,* p. 164.

143.   P. P. Bliss, "Whosoever Will," Chorus, *Sacred Songs & Solos,* ed., Ira D. Sankey (London: Marshall, Morgan & Scott), no. 389.

144.   F. W. Boreham, *Wisps of Wildfire* (New York: Abingdon Press, 1924), p. 234.

145.   Henry Drummond, *The Ideal Life* (London: Hodder & Stoughton, 1899), p. 48 says, "Some men . . . are kept from going astray by mere cowardice.   They have not character enough to lose their character."

146.   P. P. Bliss, "Daniel's Band," Chorus, *Sacred Songs & Solos,* ed., Ira D. Sankey (London: Marshall, Morgan & Scott), no. 707.

147.   B.E., arr., "None But Christ Can Satisfy," *Sacred Songs & Solos,* ed., Ira D. Sankey (London: Marshall, Morgan & Scott), no. 853.

148.   W. W. Weeks, *The Heart of God* (Nashville: Sunday School Board of the Southern Baptist Convention, 1924), p. 139.

149.   Thomas Bulfinch, *The Age of Fable* (New York: The Mershon Company), pp.37-39.

150.   Gordon Powell, *Release from Guilt and Fear* (New York: Hawthorne Books Inc., 1961), p. 87.

151.   William Barclay, *And Jesus Said* (Philadelphia: The Westminster Press, 1970), p. 181.

152.   Archibald Thomas Robertson, *Word Pictures in the New*

Testament, vol. 2 (New York: Richard R. Smith, 1930), p. 211.

153. Liddle & Scott, *A Lexicon* (Oxford: Clarendon Press, 1929), p. 786.

154. Macniele Dixon, *The Human Situation* (London: Edward Arnold Publishers, 1937), p. 147.

155. Maltbie Babcock, "This Is My Father's World," v 1, *The Hymnary* (Toronto: The Ryerson Press, 1936), no. 589.

156. George Arthur Buttrick, *The Interpreter's Bible,* vol. 1 (Nashville: Abingdon Press, 1952), p. xxi.

157. John Fawcett, "Blest Be the Tie that Binds," v 1, *The Hymnary* (Toronto: The Ryerson Press, 1936), no. 376.

158. Roy Angell, *Iron Shoes* (Nashville: The Broadman Press, 1953), pp. 58-59.

159. John Fawcett, "The Tie That Binds," v 3.

160. William Barclay, *The Gospel of Luke* (Philadelphia: The Westminster Press, 1956), p. 213.

161. William Barclay, *And Jesus Said* (Philadelphia: The Westminster Press, 1970), p. 186.

162   Joachim Jeremias, *The Parables of Jesus* (New York: Charles Scribner's Sons, 1955), p. 103.

163. James M. Dunn, "Reflections," *Report From the Capital,* p. 15.

164. John Oxenham, "In Christ there Is No East or West," v 1, *The Hymnary* (Toronto: The Ryerson Press, 1936), no. 252.

165. John J. Carey, "Marney and the Southern Baptists," *Review & Expositor,* vol. 80, no.1 (Winter, 1983), p. 127.

166.   John Keats, *Endymion,* bk.1, line 1.

167.   Archibald Thomas Robertson, *Word Pictures in the New Testament,* vol. 2 (New York: Richard C. Smith Inc., 1930), p. 213.

168.   Leslie Weatherhead, *Psychology, Religion and Healing* (London: Hodder & Stoughton, 1951), p. 338.

169.   John Watson [Ian Maclaren], *The Days of Auld Lang Syne* (London: Hodder & Stoughton, n.d.), n.p.

170.   Truett Rogers, "You Are Accepted" (Sermon delivered at First Baptist Church, Morgantown, WV, April 1984).

171.   Story told by Robert D. Dewey and taken from *Sunday School Quarterly* (July 23, 1973), p. 40.

172.   Robert James McCracken, "The Hope that Springs Eternal," *Pulpit Digest* (December 1961), p. 16.

173.   John S. Whale, *Victor and Victim* (Cambridge: University Press), p. 69.

174.   Ibid., p. 77.

175.   Lesslie Newbigin, *Unfinished Agenda* (Grand Rapids: William B. Eerdmans, 1985), pp. 254-55.

176.   Joseph Hart, "Come Ye Sinners," stanzas 1, 2 and 5, *The Hymnary* (Toronto: The Ryerson Press, 1936), no. 476.

177.   William Shakespeare, *The Merchant of Venice,* act 5, sc. 1, line 90.

178.   Roy W. Battenhouse, *A Companion to the Study of St. Augustine* (New York: Oxford University Press, 1955), p. 39.

179.   Edwin T. Dahlberg, *I Pick Up Hitchhikers* (Valley Forge: Judson Press, 1978), pp. 30-32.

180.   James Gordon Gilkey, "Goings Out and Comings In," *Best Sermons, 1951-52* (New York: The Macmillan Co., 1952), pp. 141-42.

181.   J. M. Wigner, "Come to the Savior Now," *The Hymnary* (Toronto: The Ryerson Press, 1936), no. 472.

ABOUT THE WRITER

Samuel Robert Weaver is a Canadian by birth, a clergyman by profession, a sometime resident of both Canada and the United States by choice. Educated at McGill University (B.A.), McMaster University (M.A.), McMaster Divinity College (B.D.), and Princeton Theological Seminary (Th.D.), Weaver served churches in Quebec, Ontario and Saskatchewan before crossing the border to minister to Churches in Princeton, New Jersey, and St. Albans, West Virginia. During his ministry his sermons were published in *The Canadian Baptist,* the *Watchman-Examiner, The Pulpit Digest,* and in *The Ministers Manual.*

Married to the former Elizabeth Mable Beatty, the Weavers have six children all of whom reside in the United States. Weaver and his wife are now retired and live in Port Dover, Ontario, Canada.